DISCIPLES PATH.

THE JOURNEY

VOLUME 1

LifeWay Press®
Nashville, Tennessee

DISCIPLES PATH

Disciples Path is a series of studies founded on Jesus' model of discipleship. Created by experienced disciple makers across the nation, it offers an intentional pathway for transformational discipleship and a way to help followers of Christ move from new disciples to mature disciple makers. Each study in the series is built on the principles of modeling, practicing, and multiplying:

- Leaders model the life of a biblical disciple.

- Disciples follow and practice from the leader.

- Disciples become disciple makers and multiply through the *Disciples Path*.

Each study in the series has been written and approved by disciple makers for small groups and one-on-one settings.

MINISTRY GRID
training made simple

For helps on how to use *Disciples Path,* tips on how to better lead groups, or additional ideas for leading this study, visit: *ministrygrid.com/web/disciplespath*

© 2016 LifeWay Press®

No part of this work may be reproduced or transmitted in any form or by any means, electronic or mechanical, including photocopying and recording, or by any information storage or retrieval system, except as may be expressly permitted in writing by the publisher. Requests for permission should be addressed in writing to LifeWay Press®; One LifeWay Plaza; Nashville, TN 37234-0152.

Item: 005788830 • ISBN: 978-1-4300-6225-7

Eric Geiger
Vice President, LifeWay Resources

Philip Nation
Director of Content Development

Sam O'Neal, Joel Polk
Content Editors

Michael Kelley
Director, Groups Publishing

We believe that the Bible has God for its author; salvation for its end; and truth, without any mixture of error, for its matter and that all Scripture is totally true and trustworthy. To review LifeWay's doctrinal guideline, visit *lifeway.com/doctrinalguideline.*

All Scripture quotations are taken from the Christian Standard Bible®, Copyright 2017 by Holman Bible Publishers. Used by permission.

To order additional copies of this resource, write to LifeWay Resources Customer Service; One LifeWay Plaza; Nashville, TN 37234-0113; fax 615.251.5933; call toll free 800.458.2772; order online at *lifeway.com;* email *orderentry@lifeway.com;* or visit the LifeWay Christian Store serving you.

Printed in the United States of America

Groups Ministry Publishing; LifeWay Resources
One LifeWay Plaza; Nashville, TN 37234-0152

CONTENTS

HOW TO USE THIS RESOURCE

Welcome to *Disciples Path: The Journey*. Over the course of one year you'll explore biblical stories of disciple-making and replication in order to gain a better understanding of what it means to follow Christ. As you get started, consider the following guides and suggestions for making the most of this experience.

GROUP DISCUSSION

Because the process of discipleship always involves at least two people—the leader and the disciple— each session of *Disciples Path: The Journey* includes a practical plan for group engagement and discussion.

This plan includes the following steps:

- **GET STARTED.** The first section of the group material helps you ease into the discussion by starting on common ground. You'll begin by reflecting on the previous session and your recent experiences as a disciple. After spending time in prayer, you'll find a practical illustration to help you launch into the main topic of the current session.

- **THE STORY.** While using *Disciples Path: The Journey*, you'll find opportunities to engage the Bible through both story and teaching. That's why the group time for each session features two main sections: **Know the Story** and **Unpack the Story. Know the Story** introduces a biblical text and includes follow-up questions for brief discussion. It's recommended that your group encounter the biblical text by reading it out loud. **Unpack the Story** includes practical teaching material and discussion questions—both designed to help you engage the truths contained in the biblical text. To make the most of your experience, use the provided material as a launching point for deeper conversation. As you read through the teaching material and engage the questions as a group, be thinking of how the truths you're exploring will impact your everyday life.

- **ENGAGE.** The group portion of each session ends with an activity designed to help you practice the biblical principles introduced in **Know the Story** and more fully explored in **Unpack the Story.** This part of the group time often appeals to different learning styles and will push you to engage the text at a personal level.

INDIVIDUAL DISCOVERY

Each session of *Disciples Path: The Journey* also includes content for individual use during the time between group gatherings. This content is divided into three categories:

⬆ **Worship:** features content for worship and devotion. These activities provide opportunities for you to connect with God in meaningful ways and deepen your relationship with Him.

⬆⬅ **Personal study:** features content for personal study. These pages help you gain a deeper understanding of the truths and principles explored during the group discussion.

⬅➡ **Application:** features content for practical application. These suggestions help you take action based on the information you've learned and your encounters with God.

Note: Aside from the **Reading Plan,** the content provided in the Individual Discovery portion of each session should be considered optional. You'll get the most out of your personal study by working with your group leader to create a personalized discipleship plan using the **Weekly Activities** checklist included in each session.

ADDITIONAL SUGGESTIONS

- You'll be best prepared for each group discussion or mentoring conversation if you read the session material beforehand. A serious read will serve you most effectively, but skimming the **Get Started** and **The Story** sections will also be helpful if time is limited.

- The deeper you're willing to engage in the group discussions and individual discovery each session, the more you'll benefit from those experiences. Don't hold back, and don't be afraid to ask questions whenever necessary.

- As you explore the **Engage** portion of each session, you'll have the chance to practice different activities and spiritual disciplines. Take advantage of the chance to observe others during the group time—and to ask questions—so that you'll be prepared to incorporate these activities into your private spiritual life as well.

WHAT JUST HAPPENED?

You were created by a passionate God
who relentlessly pursued you to bring
you into His family. Welcome home.

REFLECT

In this study, we'll explore what it means to be a disciple of Jesus. You may have been a disciple of Jesus for many years, or may have recently made a decision to take a step of faith. Regardless, this decision to follow Jesus may seem like something you initiated, but God has been at work in your life and pursuing you for quite some time. Take a moment to describe some of your encounters with God.

Describe the first time you heard about God.

Describe the first time you prayed to God.

Describe a time that God may have been present and active in your life but you didn't recognize it at the time.

PRAY

One of the ways we communicate with God is through prayer. At its core, prayer is simply talking to God—telling Him what's on your heart and actively listening for His response. When you're starting out, it might feel uncomfortable, erratic, and difficult. If so, don't worry. That's normal.

Spend a few moments with God by bowing your head to acknowledge who He is. Close your eyes to block out distractions. If you need help getting started, here's a five-point prayer for guidance. We'll be looking at other approaches to prayer in the next few sessions.

- Greet God. How you address God may depend on what you want to talk to Him about. He functions in a limitless capacity: Father, Daddy, Friend, Almighty, Savior, and Redeemer.

- Tell Him what you're thankful for.

- Tell Him what you're concerned about.

- Ask Him to help you understand the elements of the study today.

- Take time to listen for His response.

INTRODUCTION

New creation. Saved. Born again. Redeemed.

These are just a few ways the Bible describes conversion, which is our response to the great gift of salvation, through which we're forgiven for being less than God created us to be. Jesus called His original disciples by saying, "Follow me," and He later explained that we must be "born again." But what do those terms mean?

Ultimately, salvation, or being born again, means leaving your old ways behind and trusting God. He initiated a relationship with you and offered you a way to experience that relationship. And you responded. You've turned from your old life and turned toward God. You've been freed from sin and made right in His eyes. And you've been rescued from Satan, the enemy of God, and adopted into God's family.

Read 2 Corinthians 5:17. What old things are you hoping will go away?

What new things do you hope Jesus will bring to your life?

The way we experience God's grace and mercy looks different for different people. Perhaps it felt as though you turned a corner in your life and discovered God right in front of you, or maybe you felt like He chased you down and caught you from behind. Regardless of how you describe your own journey, all such stories share a few things in common—a change in what you believe, a transfer of loyalty, and a reversal of direction. God forgives, saves, restores, and reconciles.

Are there people you've "followed" over the course of your life? There are a few ways you can follow someone or something. You can follow people on social media. You can follow a favorite sports team or celebrity gossip. You can follow a philosophy or an idea. But when the Creator of the universe—God in the person of Jesus Christ—says, "Follow me" (Matt. 4:19), we intuitively know that's something much different.

KNOW THE STORY

One day as Simon Peter was cleaning his fishing nets after an unsuccessful day on the water, Jesus climbed into his boat. Jesus had offered some unusual instructions for Simon Peter, and the resulting miracle brought the fisherman to his knees. He told Simon Peter to push back out into the water and to cast out his net again. He did as Jesus said, and the net filled up with fish. After the massive amount of fish began to sink his boat, Simon Peter realized who Jesus was and it brought him to his knees.

> [4] When he had finished speaking, he said to Simon, "Put out into deep water and let down your nets for a catch." [5] "Master," Simon replied, "we've worked hard all night long and caught nothing. But if you say so, I'll let down the nets." [6] When they did this, they caught a great number of fish, and their nets began to tear. [7] So they signaled to their partners in the other boat to come and help them; they came and filled both boats so full that they began to sink. [8] When Simon Peter saw this, he fell at Jesus's knees and said, "Go away from me, because I'm a sinful man, Lord!" [9] For he and all those with him were amazed at the catch of fish they had taken, [10] and so were James and John, Zebedee's sons, who were Simon's partners. "Don't be afraid," Jesus told Simon. "From now on you will be catching people." [11] Then they brought the boats to land, left everything, and followed him.
> LUKE 5:4-11

What are some practical examples of what it looks like to follow Jesus in your life?

What makes it difficult to follow Jesus? What makes it easier?

Being a Christian isn't about following rules; it's about following a Person. It's not about asking Jesus to follow us but about deciding to follow Him. Jesus doesn't stand in a far off place and demand that we get our act together before approaching Him; rather, He invades the reality of our lives and beckons us into a life larger than our own.

Following Jesus is ultimately about doing what Jesus did the way that He did it. It's that simple. We love the people He loved, serve the people He served, and do the things He did. We strive to replicate His character, ways, and mission.

UNPACK THE STORY

Creation. Fall. Redemption. Re-creation. These four events represent the great story of God—the gospel story. It was the story Simon Peter was swept into and it's the story you have now been swept into. Our lives make sense only as we understand them against this backdrop. Let's examine each of these events.

CREATION—In the beginning, God created. At the sound of His voice, galaxies were hurled into orbit and the smallest organisms were established. Water was pure, creation was untainted, and life was perfect. Then God created man and woman. Fashioned with His own hands and infused with His own breath, He created Adam and Eve to be in relationship with Him and to be stewards of His creation.

Why do you think it's important to know God as Creator?

> God created man and woman. Fashioned with His own hands and infused with His own breath, He created Adam and Eve to be in relationship with Him and to be stewards of His creation.

FALL—Then, the Villain entered the story. Twisting the words of God and promising a better life, Satan planted a seed of unbelief in the woman's heart. Eve doubted the goodness and trustworthiness of God and reached for the very thing that compromised her relationship with Him. Adam and Eve believed a lie, turned against God, and pursued a story of their own making which left them separated from their Creator. Sin entered the world through humanity and everything broke. And that's what sin is: turning away from God's desire with actions, attitudes, or thoughts.

What have you been taught about the nature and consequences of sin?

How do you see sin's effects today?

Violence. War. Dishonesty. Greed. Sickness. The perfect creation became overgrown with evil, chaos, and despair. It was soon overrun with people who searched for meaning and salvation through selfish ambition. The world needed a Savior.

For centuries, God pursued His people. He gave them leaders, prophets, and priests to guide them into relationship with Him. But over and over, the people became distracted and turned their attention to man-made gods. God's complete redemption was yet to come.

REDEMPTION—In order to reverse the disastrous effects of sin, to free people from the clutches of the Villain, and to restore people to God the Father, Jesus came to the earth with His eyes on the cross. Fully God, Jesus made the perfect sacrifice to pay the debt of our sin and to cancel the curse of death on our lives. Fully human, Jesus was able to completely represent man before God. Redemption had come. On the third day, Jesus rose from the grave to conquer sin and death once and for all.

What is significant to you about Jesus being both fully God and fully man?

RE-CREATION—The story didn't end at the empty tomb; it had just begun. The great story of God would explode across the globe and change the hearts and lives of men and women for all eternity. All creation is moving toward a great day when Jesus returns and fixes everything that's broken once and for all.

All creation is moving toward a great day when Jesus returns and fixes everything that's broken once and for all.

When you read the overarching story of God, is there anything that surprises you? Why?

ENGAGE

Here's a simple description of what it means to follow Jesus: doing what Jesus did the way that He did it. Read Philippians 2:5-11 together, aloud. Using this passage as a guide, make a list with the space provided of the attributes and actions of Jesus that His followers should imitate.

Philippians 2:5-11	Attributes and actions of Jesus

⁵ Adopt the same attitude as that of Christ Jesus, ⁶ who, existing in the form of God, did not consider equality with God as something to be exploited. ⁷ Instead he emptied himself by assuming the form of a servant, taking on the likeness of humanity. And when he had come as a man, ⁸ he humbled himself by becoming obedient to the point of death—even to death on a cross. ⁹ For this reason God highly exalted him and gave him the name that is above every name, ¹⁰ so that at the name of Jesus every knee will bow—in heaven and on earth and under the earth— ¹¹ and every tongue will confess that Jesus Christ is Lord, to the glory of God the Father.

....

....

....

....

....

....

....

....

....

....

....

....

PRAYER REQUESTS:

....

....

....

....

....

....

In addition to studying God's Word, work with your group leader to create a plan for personal study, worship, and application between now and the next session. Select from the following optional activities to match your personal preferences and available time.

⬆ Worship

☑ Read your Bible. Complete the reading plan on page 14.

☐ Spend time with God by engaging the devotional experience on page 15.

☐ Connect with God each day. Start each morning with the five-part prayer included in the beginning of this study. At the end of every day, reflect on the times you felt closest to God and when you felt most distant.

➡⬅ Personal Study

☐ Read and interact with "How Jesus Came" on page 16.

☐ Read and interact with "Why Jesus Came" on page 18.

⬅➡ Application

☐ Connect with your church. Attend a church worship service and take notes as the pastor teaches from the Bible.

☐ Connect with others. Seek out someone of the same gender who has also recently come into a relationship with Christ. Discuss your individual experiences over dinner or coffee.

☐ Memorize 2 Corinthians 5:17: "Therefore, if anyone is in Christ, he is a new creation; the old has passed away, and see, the new has come!" Share this newly memorized verse with two different people.

☐ Spend time journaling. Benjamin Franklin said, "The shortest pencil is longer than the longest memory." Keeping a record of the things you are learning and the ways God is working in your life is a great way to track your spiritual growth. Each day, write down one thing you are learning about God.

☐ Other:

 **WORSHIP**

READING PLAN

Begin reading through the Gospel of Mark this week. Use the space provided to record your thoughts and responses.

Day 1
Mark 1:1-15

Day 2
Mark 1:16-28

Day 3
Mark 1:29-45

Day 4
Mark 2:1-17

Day 5
Mark 2:18-28

Day 6
Mark 3:1-19

Day 7
Mark 3:20-35

HOMECOMING

The first words preached by Jesus are found in Matthew 4:17, where He said: "Repent, because the kingdom of heaven has come near." It's also the foundation for the first sermon preached in the Book of Acts, when Peter declared: "Repent and be baptized, each of you, in the name of Jesus Christ for the forgiveness of your sins, and you will receive the gift of the Holy Spirit" (Acts 2:38).

When we hear "repent," we often think it includes punishment or correction. But this word gives life. It doesn't mean "get your act together" or "clean up your behavior" so much as it means to simply turn around: to turn from sin and turn to God. It implies readiness. It results in a complete change of mind, heart, and action, but the first step is to turn around and see God.

> *Repentance isn't something we do in order to come to God, it's simply our coming to God. What is your reaction to this statement?*

> *Take a moment and read Luke 15:11-24. What are your initial thoughts from the parable of the lost son?*

This story follows the journey of a man who strays far from home and far from the man he was destined to be. But eventually he backs away from his depraved life, turns around, and walks back home. That's what repentance is. It's homecoming. And when we return home, we don't find a father who is angry or eager to say "I told you so." Rather, we see a Father who runs to us. Jesus doesn't call us to repentance to just change our behavior. He changes our hearts and where we rest our heads. It's about who or what we are trusting in.

> *Before trusting in the work done by Christ on the cross, what were the things you trusted in?*

The journey home begins with repentance at the cross. The greatest plot twist in history was God Himself coming to earth to deal with sin. At the cross, Jesus took all our sin onto Himself and paid our debt. This paved the way for us to go back home. Because of this we know we were created by a passionate Father in heaven who relentlessly pursues His children to bring them back to the family. Welcome home.

> *Give an example of an area in your life in which you need to change direction.*

HOW JESUS CAME

> For a child will be born for us, a son will be given to us, and the government will be on his shoulders. He will be named Wonderful Counselor, Mighty God, Eternal Father, Prince of Peace.
> ISAIAH 9:6

God made a promise at the very beginning of time that He would make things right, and that's what the coming of Jesus was about. Jesus came not just to teach moral lessons or to set good examples. He came to liberate, make things right, and start a revolution. Let's look at four of the ways Jesus came to us.

1. Jesus left His rightful place in heaven and came into the chaos of humanity.

In a stone feeding trough for animals, the voice of God was heard in the cry of an infant. He came dressed in the skin of His own creation, subjected Himself to the care of His own creation, and fixed His eyes on the salvation of humanity. He turned water into wine. He showed mercy to sexually promiscuous women. He healed the sick. He commanded dead men to walk out of their graves. He loved and showed honor to the scum of society.

> But we do see Jesus—made lower than the angels for a short time so that by God's grace he might taste death for everyone—crowned with glory and honor because he suffered death.
> HEBREWS 2:9

Have you ever thought of Jesus in these terms? How does the way Christ came to Earth encourage you as we live in a culture tainted by sin?

2. Jesus came as a man.

He was born; He had a physical body and physical limitations; He expressed human emotions; He grew physically, emotionally, and relationally (see Matt. 1:18; John 4:6; John 19:28). Because He was fully human, He's able to represent us, to pay our penalty, to mediate for us before God, to serve as our example, and to identify with us.

> [7] Instead he emptied himself by assuming the form of a servant, taking on the likeness of humanity. And when he had come as a man, [8] he humbled himself by becoming obedient to the point of death—even to death on a cross.
> PHILIPPIANS 2:7-8

3. Jesus also came as God.

His birth was supernatural. He claimed to be God, God declared him to be God, and even the demons recognized Him to be God. He displayed attributes of deity such as working miracles and forgiving sins (see Matt. 1:18; Col. 2:9). Because He was fully God, He was able to offer a perfect sacrifice.

> And we know that the Son of God has come and has given us understanding so that we may know the true one. We are in the true one—that is, in his Son Jesus Christ. He is the true God and eternal life.
> 1 JOHN 5:20

Is it difficult for you to grasp the thought of Jesus as fully God and fully man? Why or why not?

Why is it important that He is both?

4. Jesus came to serve, sacrifice, and save.

Romans 5:8 declares, "But God proves his own love for us in that while we were still sinners, Christ died for us." He is uniquely designed to represent people to God and God to people. Because He is fully human, He can offer the sacrifice on our behalf. Because He is fully God, He can offer the perfect sacrifice.

> [9] God's love was revealed among us in this way: God sent his one and only Son into the world so that we might live through him. [10] Love consists in this: not that we loved God, but that he loved us and sent his Son to be the atoning sacrifice for our sins.
> 1 JOHN 4:9-10

What's your reaction to the idea that salvation isn't found in what we do for God but in what He has done for us?

PERSONAL STUDY

WHY JESUS CAME

Being a Christian isn't about what you do for God; it's about what God has already done for you. Jesus paid our debt, freed us from sin and death, and reconciled us to God and others. Jesus divinely disrupted and reversed the story of humanity. On the cross, our guilt, the bondage of sin, and our separation from God were reconciled. Let's take a moment to explore those terms on a deeper level.

Guilt: Everyone understands words like "guilt" and "debt." But what many don't realize is that we're born into much less-than-favorable standing with God—by association with Adam. We're literally "born into" guilt and bondage. But Jesus paid a debt that He didn't owe and that we couldn't pay so that the charges of sin are canceled against us. Through Jesus, we experience forgiveness and cleansing. This is called *propitiation*.

> He made the one who did not know sin to be sin for us, so that in him we might become the righteousness of God.
> 2 CORINTHIANS 5:21

Journal your thoughts on the concept of guilt.

Bondage: Jesus defeated the power of sin and death on the cross, liberating us from its grip on our lives and granting us eternal life in Him. Through Jesus, we are freed from sin. This is called *redemption*.

> 22 But now, since you have been set free from sin and have become enslaved to God, you have your fruit, which results in sanctification—and the outcome is eternal life! 23 For the wages of sin is death, but the gift of God is eternal life in Christ Jesus our Lord.
> ROMANS 6:22-23

Journal your thoughts on the concept of bondage.

Separation: Jesus removed the wedge between us and God and made a way for us to have a relationship with Him. Through Christ, we are reunited with God. This is called *reconciliation*.

> [10] For if, while we were enemies, we were reconciled to God through the death of his Son, then how much more, having been reconciled, will we be saved by his life. [11] And not only that, but we also rejoice in God through our Lord Jesus Christ, through whom we have now received this reconciliation.
> ROMANS 5:10-11

Journal your thoughts on the concept of separation.

Respond to the following statement: Jesus' work on the cross pays for our sin and removes our guilt. It liberates us from bondage and restores our relationship with God.

Which term do you not fully understand? Who will you seek out this week to gain a better understanding of this?

Jesus didn't die on the cross to give us comfort and safety. Some people sell salvation like it's an insurance plan or a safety net. Unfortunately, we sometimes think that coming to God means that everything will be OK. Life will get better. Sometimes, it gets worse. We aren't promised that everything will be OK; we're promised His presence. He doesn't promise to keep us safe; rather, He invites us into a dangerous story to be proclaimers of hope in the midst of a very unsafe world.

Jesus didn't die to make us safe but to make us proclaimers of hope in an unsafe world. How might this affect the way you view life?

THE CENTRALITY OF CHRIST

Christians are people who've had a spiritual revolution placing Jesus at the center of their lives.

REFLECT

We examined in the previous session the overarching story of God and His calling us into it. We saw how Jesus' death paid for our sin, freed us from bondage, and restored our relationship with God. We also learned that being a follower of Christ is doing what Jesus did the way that He did it.

Which of the assignments did you explore this week? How did it go?

What did you learn or experience while reading the Bible?

What questions would you like to ask?

PRAY

Begin this session by connecting with God through prayer. Use the following guidelines as you speak with Him together:

- Thank God for His goodness and grace in saving you though His Son, Jesus Christ.

- Confess that you are still sinful and need His grace just as much as you did the day you were saved.

- Ask God to bring the hearts of the individuals in your group together over the next few weeks.

INTRODUCTION

The Bible uses a construction analogy to describe followers of Christ, saying that Jesus is our "cornerstone" (see Eph. 2:19-22). For a builder, the cornerstone of a building was central to its construction. It was both the strongest stone and the straightest as every other stone in the building was aligned by it. The cornerstone was laid first. If the cornerstone was straight, every other stone in the building naturally ended up in its proper place. If its angle was even slightly off, every other stone was off.

The Bible says Jesus is the cornerstone of a Christian's life. His place in our lives isn't decided by anything else. A Christian is a person who says, "the place of everything in my life is negotiable but Jesus."

A modern analogy would be the universe. Before Copernicus, the universe was interpreted as revolving around ourselves (Earth). Copernicus discovered that something much larger and more powerful was at the center of our universe—the sun—and that everything else revolved around it. This sparked a revolution in which all understanding of the solar system had to be reworked around a new center.

This is exactly what happens when someone becomes a Christian. Having realized that Jesus is at the center of the universe, we must rework our understanding of everything else around Him as the new center. This is how everything in our lives finds its proper place. A Christian is a person in the midst of a spiritual Copernican revolution.

What are some fears or confusions you have about "reworking our lives around a new center"?

What stands out the most as you learn about the spiritual Copernican revolution?

KNOW THE STORY

The Gospel of Luke describes a man for whom Jesus had become central.

¹ He entered Jericho and was passing through. ² There was a man named Zacchaeus who was a chief tax collector, and he was rich. ³ He was trying to see who Jesus was, but he was not able because of the crowd, since he was a short man. ⁴ So running ahead, he climbed up a sycamore tree to see Jesus, since he was about to pass that way. ⁵ When Jesus came to the place, he looked up and said to him, "Zacchaeus, hurry and come down because today it is necessary for me to stay at your house." ⁶ So he quickly came down and welcomed him joyfully. ⁷ All who saw it began to complain, "He's gone to stay with a sinful man." ⁸ But Zacchaeus stood there and said to the Lord, "Look, I'll give half of my possessions to the poor, Lord. And if I have extorted anything from anyone, I'll pay back four times as much." ⁹ "Today salvation has come to this house," Jesus told him, "because he too is a son of Abraham. ¹⁰ For the Son of Man has come to seek and to save the lost."
LUKE 19:1-10

What was central to your identity before you became a Christian? What defined you?

Zacchaeus was wealthy because he extorted money from people as a tax collector. But that changed when he met Jesus. Zacchaeus' focus on money shifted (v. 8)—Jesus was the new center of his life.

Why do you think Zacchaeus—a wealthy man by all indications—would choose to give it all up to make Jesus central in his life?

UNPACK THE STORY

CENTRAL TO MY IDENTITY

Zacchaeus was a hated man. For the most part, tax collectors in his time were hated men in a Jewish community for two main reasons:

1. They were notorious thieves who gained their wealth by extorting money from taxpayers. They were hated for their thievery.

2. They were also known as traitors to their culture as Roman governors would choose Jewish men as tax-collectors in Jewish regions. They were hated for betraying their ethnic community to ally with the pagan Roman government.

Judging from what you know about his story, what do you think Zacchaeus thought about himself before encountering Jesus?

What did Zacchaeus' lifestyle suggest about his identity and motivation?

When we become Christians, Jesus redefines us as He becomes central to our identity and view of ourselves.

Zacchaeus had always been hated, but what caused Zacchaeus to change was the whole new view of himself that Jesus gave him: he was loved and accepted by Christ.

Similarly, when we become Christians, Jesus redefines us as He becomes central to our identity and our view of ourselves. For Christians, the defining moment of our lives is Jesus' crucifixion on the cross. Everything the cross reveals about us is the most true and important information we can know about ourselves.

Why is it so important to understand that we are loved and accepted by Christ?

CENTRAL TO WHAT I DO

Jesus must also be central to what we do. He puts everything else in life into its proper place.

The story of Zacchaeus shows that there's only one position Jesus will occupy in a person's life: a central position. When Jesus became central to Zacchaeus, we're shown that it dramatically altered his actions in two areas: people and money.

Because Jesus had become central, Zacchaeus' treatment of people and money were now taking their cues from Jesus. As Christians, we approach every area of our lives with the intent of aligning them to Jesus.

What's the most difficult part of this realignment?

What's the most freeing part of approaching life with this new perspective?

Take a few minutes to read Luke 18:18-23. Discuss what you think was going on in the ruler's heart that kept him from obeying Jesus' challenge.

Jesus saw the ruler's heart and asked if he'd be willing to get rid of his money and reorient his entire life. The man went away sad because he didn't want the decisions he made with his money to revolve around Jesus. Because his money was central, the ruler saw Jesus as secondary.

Because Jesus had become central, Zacchaeus' treatment of people and money were now taking their cues from Jesus.

ENGAGE

Take some time to go below the surface and engage the text at a different level. Read Acts 7:54-60 and Luke 23:32-46 together. Circle the similarities you find between how Jesus died and how Stephen died.

54 When they heard these things, they were enraged and gnashed their teeth at him. 55 Stephen, full of the Holy Spirit, gazed into heaven. He saw the glory of God, and Jesus standing at the right hand of God. 56 He said, "Look, I see the heavens opened and the Son of Man standing at the right hand of God!" 57 They yelled at the top of their voices, covered their ears, and together rushed against him. 58 They dragged him out of the city and began to stone him. And the witnesses laid their garments at the feet of a young man named Saul. 59 While they were stoning Stephen, he called out: "Lord Jesus, receive my spirit!" 60 He knelt down and cried out with a loud voice, "Lord, do not hold this sin against them!" And after saying this, he died.
ACTS 7:54-60

32 Two others—criminals—were also led away to be executed with him. 33 When they arrived at the place called The Skull, they crucified him there, along with the criminals, one on the right and one on the left. 34 Then Jesus said, "Father, forgive them, because they do not know what they are doing." And they divided his clothes and cast lots. 35 The people stood watching, and even the leaders were scoffing: "He saved others; let him save himself if this is God's Messiah, the Chosen One!" 36 The soldiers also mocked him. They came offering him sour wine 37 and said, "If you are the King of the Jews, save yourself!" 38 An inscription was above him: THIS IS THE KING OF THE JEWS. 39 Then one of the criminals hanging there began to yell insults at him: "Aren't you the Messiah? Save yourself and us!" 40 But the other answered, rebuking him: "Don't you even fear God, since you are undergoing the same punishment? 41 We are punished justly, because we're getting back what we deserve for the things we did, but this man has done nothing wrong." 42 Then he said, "Jesus, remember me when you come into your kingdom." 43 And he said to him, "Truly I tell you, today you will be with me in paradise." 44 It was now about noon, and darkness came over the whole land until three, 45 because the sun's light failed. The curtain of the sanctuary was split down the middle. 46 And Jesus called out with a loud voice, "Father, into your hands I entrust my spirit." Saying this, he breathed his last.
LUKE 23:32-46

How do these two passages contribute to your understanding of the centrality of Christ?

WEEKLY ACTIVITIES

In addition to studying God's Word, work with your group leader to create a plan for personal study, worship, and application between now and the next session. Select from the following optional activities to match your personal preferences and available time.

↑ Worship

☑ Read your Bible. Complete the reading plan on page 28.

☐ Spend time with God by engaging the devotional experience on page 29.

☐ Connect with God each day. Every morning this week, commit several minutes to prayer. Ask God to help you solidify Jesus as central to your identity. Use the following prayer as a starting point. "Dear Father, because of Jesus, there is nothing I did yesterday that made You love me less and there is nothing I could do today to make You love me more."

➡ ⬅ Personal Study

☐ Read and interact with "Central to My Identity" on page 30.

☐ Read and interact with "Central to What I Do" on page 32.

⬅ ➡ Application

☐ Connect with your church. As an expression of the centrality of Jesus in your finances, give to your local church this week.

☐ Memorize Philippians 1:21: "For me, to live is Christ and to die is gain."

☐ Do something for someone. Find a practical way to help someone who cannot help you in return this week.

☐ Place Jesus at the center. Make a budget and a weekly schedule that reflects Jesus as central to your finances and to your usage of time.

☐ Other:

WORSHIP

READING PLAN

Continue reading through the Gospel of Mark this week. Use the space provided to record your thoughts and responses.

Day 1
Mark 4:1-20

Day 2
Mark 4:21-41

Day 3
Mark 5:1-20

Day 4
Mark 5:21-43

Day 5
Mark 6:1-13

Day 6
Mark 6:14-29

Day 7
Mark 6:30-44

INCREASINGLY CENTRAL

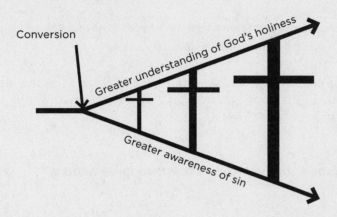

This is a visual representation of the Christian life and the process by which the cross becomes increasingly central in our thinking. The chart moves chronologically from left to right, and the point of divergence is when someone becomes a Christian. The longer someone is a Christian, two things happen: they have a deeper understanding of God's holiness and of their own sinfulness.

This is why Paul, one of the holiest men who ever lived, referred to himself as "the chief of sinners." As these two awarenesses grow, one's view of the cross gets ever larger and larger. Someone who has been a Christian for two decades will be far more aware of how much the cross did for them than someone who has been a Christian for two days. As a person's view of the cross grows, this naturally results in attributes like thankfulness, gratitude, love, mercy, justice, etc. The Christian's character is now being transformed into the image of Jesus. This is a key aspect of how Jesus becomes increasingly central in a Christian's thinking, feeling, and acting.

In the time that you've understood what Jesus has done for you on the cross and giving your life to Him in response, have you seen Jesus become increasingly central in your life? Explain.

Do you see the ugliness of your sin any more than you did when you first became a Christian? How so?

CENTRAL TO MY IDENTITY

In the story of Zacchaeus, Jesus never commanded him to repay those he'd stolen from or to give to the poor. Zacchaeus made that decision on his own. Take a look:

> But Zacchaeus stood there and said to the Lord, "Look, I'll give half of my possessions to the poor, Lord. And if I have extorted anything from anyone, I'll pay back four times as much."
> LUKE 19:8

What do you think motivated Zacchaeus to these actions?

What did Jesus' actions communicate to Zacchaeus about his identity?

Is there a moment in your life—a failure, success, etc.—that you have allowed to define you until now? For Christians, the defining moments are Jesus' death for us on the cross and His resurrection. Because of these moments, we find our identity in Him. What once defined us has now been erased and replaced with righteousness, love, and forgiveness.

> God presented [Jesus] to demonstrate his righteousness at the present time, so that he would be righteous and declare righteous the one who has faith in Jesus.
> ROMANS 3:26

> [6] For while we were still helpless, at the right time, Christ died for the ungodly. [7] For rarely will someone die for a just person—though for a good person perhaps someone might even dare to die. [8] But God proves his own love for us in that while we were still sinners, Christ died for us. [9] How much more then, since we have now been declared righteous by his blood, will we be saved through him from wrath. [10] For if, while we were enemies, we were reconciled to God through the death of his Son, then how much more, having been reconciled, will we be saved by his life. [11] And not only that, but we also rejoice in God through our Lord Jesus Christ, through whom we have now received this reconciliation.
> ROMANS 5:6-11

How do these two passages describe our identity in Jesus?

Look at the following case studies and answer the questions attached to each.

CASE STUDY #1: Someone who grew up in a strict, morally conservative family thinks, *I am a good person.*

What is this person making central to their identity?

What would it look like for this person to make Jesus central to their identity?

CASE STUDY #2: Someone who was abused as a child has spent their whole life thinking, *I am dirty.*

What is this person making central to their identity?

What would it look like for this person to make Jesus central to their identity?

CASE STUDY #3: Someone wrestling with both the gospel and their sexuality says, "I don't know if I can become a Christian because I am gay."

What is this person making central to their identity?

What would it look like for this person to make Jesus central to their identity?

Examine your own story. What are practical things you can do to make Jesus central in your thinking about yourself?

CENTRAL TO WHAT I DO

Alarm. Protein. Five miles. Shower. Clothes. Coffee spill. Change clothes. Breakfast. Traffic delay. Meeting. Class. Emails. Lunch across town. More meetings. More classes. Traffic delay. Groceries. Errands. Home. Dinner. Homework. Chores. Emails. News. Bed. Repeat.

What does your day look like? Your life may be shockingly similar to the routine listed above. It may be even more hectic. Life is busy. And it will always be filled with things that compete with Jesus for your attention.

What things in your life are competing with Jesus for centrality in your heart?

What are symptoms that something besides Jesus is central in your living and decision making?

^{5} Trust in the LORD with all your heart,
and do not rely on your own understanding;
^{6} in all your ways know him,
and he will make your paths straight.
PROVERBS 3:5-6

Read Proverbs 3:5-6 above. Since becoming a Christian, how have you specifically started trusting God? How are you still not trusting Him?

What does it mean "in all your ways know him"?

Take a few moments and examine what it looks like to make Jesus central in the following four areas of your own life. Don't hold back. Answer the questions for each area honestly.

RELATIONSHIPS:

What are you doing to make Jesus more central to this area of your life?

In what ways are you failing to make Jesus more central to this area of your life?

FINANCES:

What are you doing to make Jesus more central to this area of your life?

In what ways are you failing to make Jesus more central to this area of your life?

TIME / SCHEDULE:

What are you doing to make Jesus more central to this area of your life?

In what ways are you failing to make Jesus more central to this area of your life?

SEX:

What are you doing to make Jesus more central to this area of your life?

In what ways are you failing to make Jesus more central to this area of your life?

FOLLOWING JESUS IN BAPTISM

The act of baptism is the corporate affirmation of the transformation that has taken place in one's life.

REFLECT

We saw in the previous session that Jesus is the central figure in human history and the most important person who ever lived. Jesus is both fully human and fully God, which is why He alone can provide salvation for all people. We also saw that living as a disciple of Jesus means making Him central in all that we are and central in everything we do.

As you prepare to dive deeper into the practice of baptism, take a moment to reflect on your experiences in recent days.

Which of the assignments did you explore this week? How did it go?

What did you learn or experience while reading the Bible?

What questions would you like to ask?

PRAY

Begin this session by connecting with God through prayer. Use the following guidelines as you speak with Him together:

- Thank God for the opportunities you have each day to obey His Word as you follow Him.

- Ask for a firm understanding of what it means to obey God through the ordinance of baptism.

- Pray that God would be continually glorified through the consistent practice of baptism in your church and community.

INTRODUCTION

There aren't many people who don't appreciate a good holiday. And in today's world, the best holidays are the ones that combine celebration of an event or an ideal with an extra layer of symbolism and participation. These are the holidays that encourage people to *commemorate* important moments from the past, rather than simply remember what happened many years ago.

Think about Thanksgiving, for example. This holiday was originally observed as a way to remember the struggles and triumphs of the earliest American settlers. In 1863—right in the middle of the American Civil War—President Abraham Lincoln delivered a proclamation that established what we currently observe as the national day of Thanksgiving on the fourth Thursday of November.

The wonderful thing about Thanksgiving, however, is that we get to participate in the holiday. We don't simply remember those settlers intellectually, nor do we stop at contemplating the value of being thankful on a philosophical level. We get to eat turkey! We get mashed potatoes and green beans and cranberry sauce and pumpkin pie! We also gather together with the people we love most so that we can feel the warmth of giving thanks on an emotional level—so that we actually *become* thankful even as we celebrate Thanksgiving.

Something similar happens within the church when we celebrate the baptism of a new disciple of Jesus. No, disciples don't get baptized every year. But the rite of baptism itself is very much a participation and a commemoration of something, rather than a simple ritual—specifically, it's a commemoration of a person's salvation.

What's one of your favorite holidays? Why?

How would you summarize your earliest impressions of baptism within the church?

As we take a deeper look at the practice of baptism within the Scriptures, we'll see that it's much more than a celebration or even a commemoration. Indeed, baptism is our first act of obedience as disciples of Christ.

KNOW THE STORY

Ritual washings and other forms of baptism were a common practice for the Jewish people before the launch of the early church. In fact, Jesus Himself was baptized by John the Baptist at the beginning of His public ministry (see Matt. 3:13-17). For that reason, the authors of the New Testament epistles included a number of instructions for incorporating the ordinance of baptism as a core practice of the church. (*Note: an "ordinance" is a spiritual practice that demonstrates a person's faith in Christ.*)

One of the most important of those instructions came from the apostle Paul in Romans 6:

[1] What should we say then? Should we continue in sin so that grace may multiply? [2] Absolutely not! How can we who died to sin still live in it? [3] Or are you unaware that all of us who were baptized into Christ Jesus were baptized into his death? [4] Therefore we were buried with him by baptism into death, in order that, just as Christ was raised from the dead by the glory of the Father, so we too may walk in newness of life. [5] For if we have been united with him in the likeness of his death, we will certainly also be in the likeness of his resurrection. [6] For we know that our old self was crucified with him so that the body ruled by sin might be rendered powerless so that we may no longer be enslaved to sin, [7] since a person who has died is freed from sin. [8] Now if we died with Christ, we believe that we will also live with him, [9] because we know that Christ, having been raised from the dead, will not die again. Death no longer rules over him. [10] For the death he died, he died to sin once for all time; but the life he lives, he lives to God. [11] So, you too consider yourselves dead to sin and alive to God in Christ Jesus.
ROMANS 6:1-11

What do you like best about these verses?

How do these verses contribute to your understanding of baptism?

UNPACK THE STORY

BAPTISM IS A PICTURE OF SALVATION

As we jump into Romans 6, we find Paul in the middle of a larger explanation about sin and salvation. In the previous chapter, Paul made the case that God's grace can provide forgiveness for all of our sins, which is the key to eternal life with Christ (see 5:18-21). In the opening verses of chapter 6, Paul made it clear that disciples who have received this grace cannot continue the sinful patterns that once defined them.

It's in the process of making this point that Paul used the practice of baptism to paint a picture of our salvation through Christ:

> ³ Or are you unaware that all of us who were baptized into Christ Jesus were baptized into his death? ⁴ Therefore we were buried with him by baptism into death, in order that, just as Christ was raised from the dead by the glory of the Father, so we too may walk in newness of life.
> ROMANS 6:3-4

"Now if we died with Christ, we believe that we will also live with him."
Romans 6:8

When new disciples are baptized within the church, they are immersed in a body of water. They are brought down into the water, just as Jesus was brought down into the grave after His death on the cross. Yet, like Jesus, the disciples don't remain in the water. They are raised out again in a symbolic representation of Christ's resurrection. That's the key to Paul's wonderful reminder in verse 8: "Now if we died with Christ, we believe that we will also live with him."

In this way, the practice of baptism serves as an object lesson that helps each disciple gain a better understanding of what it means to be saved.

In what ways can salvation be compared to a type of death?

What are some ways you've experienced a "newness of life" as a disciple of Jesus?

Baptism is a picture of salvation. It's a way to actively commemorate and celebrate our inclusion in the kingdom of God—but that's not all. The ordinance of baptism within the church is also a direct response to one of Jesus' most important commands.

BAPTISM IS A PUBLIC DECLARATION OF FAITH

So far we've addressed baptism as a personal commemoration of a disciple's personal faith in Christ, which is true. However, it's equally true that baptism also serves as a public declaration of a disciple's salvation and desire to follow Christ as a member of the church.

This public aspect of baptism is directly connected to the Great Commission, which Jesus gave to His disciples after His resurrection from the grave:

> ¹⁹ Go, therefore, and make disciples of all nations, baptizing them in the name of the Father and of the Son and of the Holy Spirit, ²⁰ teaching them to observe everything I have commanded you. And remember, I am with you always, to the end of the age.
> MATTHEW 28:19-20

Note that Jesus' words here were a commission, not a suggestion. Therefore, the baptism of new disciples is not optional; it's a command.

How do you respond to the truth that baptism is a command from Jesus?

The practice of baptism continues to benefit the church in many ways. For example, baptism is a shared experience among all disciples of Christ; it helps Christians join together as the body of Christ. Paul made that clear when he wrote: "For we were all baptized by one Spirit into one body—whether Jews or Greeks, whether slaves or free—and we were all given one Spirit to drink" (1 Cor. 12:13). Public baptisms are also a fantastic opportunity for evangelism as new disciples stand to declare in front of all witnesses their intention to follow Christ.

Baptism serves as a public declaration of a disciple's salvation and desire to follow Christ as a member of the church.

What's your "next step" regarding baptism?

How can you support the ordinance of baptism within your local church?

ENGAGE

As mentioned earlier, baptism services are a great opportunity for evangelism within a local church. This is especially true when new disciples are given the chance to publicly share their testimonies and explain their decision to follow Christ.

With that in mind, write an invitation to your church's next baptism service—something you can send to your friends, neighbors, and family members who are not yet disciples of Jesus. Use the following suggestions to help craft your invitation.

Be sure to explain what baptism is and what guests should expect during the service.

Share your testimony of becoming a disciple of Jesus and how your life has changed as a result.

Explain why you have chosen to obey Jesus through the ordinance of baptism (either in the upcoming service or previously).

Share why you hope the recipients of your invitation will attend the upcoming service.

PRAYER REQUESTS:

....

....

....

....

....

....

....

In addition to studying God's Word, work with your group leader to create a plan for personal study, worship, and application between now and the next session. Select from the following optional activities to match your personal preferences and available time.

⬆ Worship

☑ Read your Bible. Complete the reading plan on page 42.

☐ Spend time with God by engaging the devotional experience on page 43.

☐ Connect with God each day through prayer. Ask Him to reveal the next steps on your journey as a disciple of Christ.

➡⬅ Personal Study

☐ Read and interact with "The Old Testament Roots of Baptism" on page 44.

☐ Read and interact with "Three Baptisms in the New Testament" on page 46.

⬅➡ Application

☐ Determine whether you need to obey Jesus Christ through the ordinance of baptism within your church. If so, speak with a church staff member about starting that process as quickly as possible.

☐ Get to know your friends and family better by asking about their experiences with baptism. Be sure to share your own experiences in return.

☐ Make a list of friends and family members to invite to your church's next baptism service. (See the Engage activity on page 40 for more information.)

☐ Memorize Romans 6:4: "Therefore we were buried with him by baptism into death, in order that, just as Christ was raised from the dead by the glory of the Father, so we too may walk in newness of life."

☐ Other:

 **WORSHIP**

READING PLAN

Read through the following Scripture passages this week. Use the space provided to record your thoughts and responses.

Day 1
Mark 6:45-56

Day 2
Mark 7:1-13

Day 3
Mark 7:14-37

Day 4
Mark 8:1-13

Day 5
Mark 8:14-26

Day 6
Mark 8:27-38

Day 7
Mark 9:1-13

THE BAPTISM OF JESUS

As we've noted throughout this study, Jesus Christ is both fully God and fully human. And one of the blessings of Jesus' humanity is that He experienced many of the same trials and triumphs that we experience as everyday people—including baptism:

> [21] When all the people were baptized, Jesus also was baptized. As he was praying, heaven opened, [22] and the Holy Spirit descended on him in a physical appearance like a dove. And a voice came from heaven: "You are my beloved Son; with you I am well-pleased."
> LUKE 3:21-22

What strikes you as most interesting from these verses? Why?

The Father's message on this important event was no doubt encouraging to Jesus as He prepared to launch His public ministry. Yet that message should encourage all of Jesus' disciples as well.

First, the Father being "well-pleased" reminds us that all Christians have been adopted into God's family. As Paul wrote in the Book of Romans: "The Spirit himself testifies together with our spirit that we are God's children, and if children, also heirs—heirs of God and coheirs with Christ—if indeed we suffer with him so that we may also be glorified with him" (Rom. 8:16-17).

Second, the Father's declaration of being "well-pleased" reminds us that Christ has opened the door for God to be well-pleased with us, as well. When our sins are forgiven, our relationship with our perfect Creator is restored. Therefore, baptism reminds us that we have the incredible opportunity to experience God's love.

What does it mean for you, personally, to be a child of God?

How will you intentionally savor God's love today?

THE OLD TESTAMENT ROOTS OF BAPTISM

Modern disciples of Jesus typically think of baptism as a New Testament concept, and rightfully so. Throughout the history of the church, the term "baptism" has become focused specifically on the immersion of new Christians as a public declaration of their faith in Christ.

At the same time, it's helpful to remember that the practice of baptism did not originate after the death and resurrection of Christ. Baptism was a common practice in Jewish life, as well as in other cultures, before the incarnation of Jesus. In fact, Jesus Himself was baptized by John the Baptist at the beginning of His public ministry (see Matt. 3:13-17).

We can go back even farther in biblical history to identify the roots of baptism, which are present throughout the Old Testament. First, there are several key moments in the Old Testament narrative where God uses water as a form of both judgment and salvation—most notably Noah's flood and the Israelites' escape through the Red Sea.

In both of these accounts, God used water as an instrument of destruction against those living in sinful rebellion against Him. At the same time, God chose to save those faithful to Him by delivering them through the waters. Thus, both accounts serve as foundations for the practice of baptism even as they foreshadow the coming salvation made possible by the death and resurrection of Christ.

> *Read Genesis 7:11–8:14. What are your initial reactions to these verses?*

> *Read Exodus 14:15-31. How do these verses reflect both God's judgment and His salvation?*

Another key foundation for the New Testament practice of baptism is the use of water as a method of purification—of using water to symbolically wash away the corruption of sin in order to bring people back into the presence of God. Several of these instructions for purification are mentioned throughout the Old Testament law (see Lev. 14:8, for example). But one of the more prominent examples can be found in Leviticus 16, which includes instructions for the Day of Atonement—a yearly ritual in which the Israelites asked God to cleanse them from sin:

²³ "Then Aaron is to enter the tent of meeting, take off the linen garments he wore when he entered the most holy place, and leave them there. ²⁴ He will bathe his body with water in a holy place and put on his clothes. Then he must go out and sacrifice his burnt offering and the people's burnt offering; he will make atonement for himself and for the people."
LEVITICUS 16:23-24

Take a step back to read Leviticus 16:20-28. How do these verses point forward to the practice of baptism in the New Testament?

Finally, the story of Naaman in 2 Kings 5 is an effective illustration of the obedience required in the New Testament practice of baptism. In that story, Naaman was a famous commander from a foreign army who was afflicted with leprosy. Through one of his slaves, an Israelite, Naaman heard about the prophet Elisha and his power to heal disease. When Naaman finally heard from Elisha, he received what seemed like a surprising prescription:

Then Elisha sent him a messenger, who said, "Go wash seven times in the Jordan and your skin will be restored and you will be clean."
2 KINGS 5:10

At first, Naaman was insulted by this command. He believed someone as important as himself should endure something more significant than being dipped in a dirty river in order to be healed. Ultimately, however, he chose to obey the prophet's instructions. And in doing so, he was healed.

Read Naaman's full story in 2 Kings 5:1-19. What strikes you as most interesting from these verses? Why?

Why is obedience a critical element in our modern practice of baptism?

 **PERSONAL STUDY** 2

THREE BAPTISMS IN THE NEW TESTAMENT

As we've seen throughout this session, the New Testament contains a number of commands and instructions related to the practice of baptism. These commands and instructions are obviously helpful as we seek to continue the practice of baptism in the church today; however, we should also pay attention to the moments in the Scriptures that record people actually being baptized. In fact, let's look at three of those examples right now.

The first comes early in the Book of Acts. As you'll see, baptism was an important element on the Day of Atonement after Jesus' death and resurrection—the day that in many ways was the official launch of the church:

> [41] So those who accepted his message were baptized, and that day about three thousand people were added to them. [42] They devoted themselves to the apostles' teaching, to the fellowship, to the breaking of bread, and to prayer.
> ACTS 2:41-42

Verse 42 has long been viewed as an ideal picture of what Christian community should be. Not surprisingly, we want that vision to be realized in our own situations. We want the church to be a place where disciples can freely and peacefully gather together, learn together, break bread together, and pray together. Yet we must remember that baptism came first, even for the members of the earliest church. Baptism will always be our first act of obedience as the body of Christ.

What opportunities exist for you to support the practice of baptism within your church?

Continuing through the Book of Acts, the story of the Ethiopian official helps us see the importance and the immediacy of baptism as part of sharing the gospel with others.

Read Acts 8:26-40. What do you like best about these verses? Why?

How confident do you feel in teaching others about the meaning and importance of baptism?

How confident do you feel about encouraging other disciples to be baptized in obedience to Jesus' command?

Finally, the story of Cornelius's conversion in Acts 10 has long been viewed as a watershed moment in the New Testament. After all, that was the moment when the apostle Peter and other leaders of the church truly realized that the gospel was meant not just for the Israelites, but for all people.

Read Cornelius's story in Acts 10:17-43. What do these verses reveal about God?

What happened next in Cornelius's house was truly extraordinary:

> 44 While Peter was still speaking these words, the Holy Spirit came down on all those who heard the message. 45 The circumcised believers who had come with Peter were amazed because the gift of the Holy Spirit had been poured out even on the Gentiles. 46 For they heard them speaking in other tongues and declaring the greatness of God.
>
> Then Peter responded, 47 "Can anyone withhold water and prevent these people from being baptized, who have received the Holy Spirit just as we have?" 48 He commanded them to be baptized in the name of Jesus Christ. Then they asked him to stay for a few days.
> ACTS 10:44-48

These verses remind us that the transformational work of salvation is God's gift to all people—not simply to those who are like us. In addition, these verses confirm that baptism is the appropriate first step for all members of God's kingdom.

TIME WITH JESUS

You were created to know God in
a deep and personal way.

REFLECT

We looked at the act of following Jesus in baptism in the previous session. Baptism is the believer's declaration that Jesus is Lord and identification with Christ and His church. It is our first act of obedience as disciples of Jesus, and it bears witness to the world that we have moved our citizenship. We now belong to Christ and thus are part of His church.

Before we move on to this session's topic, take a moment to review what you learned throughout the week.

Which of the assignments did you explore this week? How did it go?

What did you learn or experience while reading the Bible?

What questions would you like to ask?

PRAY

Begin this session by connecting with God through prayer. Use the following guidelines as you speak with Him together:

- Thank God for His presence in your life this week.

- Ask Him to help you set aside any distractions you're experiencing now so that you can focus on His Word.

- Ask Him to speak with you as you study the Bible today.

INTRODUCTION

We live in a celebrity-obsessed culture. From supermarket magazines to gossip websites to social media, people today are desperate to know what celebrities are up to. We want to know what celebrities are wearing. We want to know which celebrities are dating other celebrities. We want to know where celebrities are dining, shopping, and watching sports. And, more often than not, we've been given round-the-clock access to all of those details and more.

The root of our obsession with celebrities is a desire to connect with something larger than ourselves. In fact, the root of our obsession with celebrities is a desire to connect with God. As created beings, we're born with an instinctive need to know and be known by our Creator. All of us were created to know God in a deep and personal way.

Don't let that truth slip away: you were created to know God in a deep and personal way.

And here's the wonderful news: you can! You may never have a meaningful connection with a cultural celebrity, but as a disciple of Jesus you have access to something immeasurably better—a daily relationship with the Creator.

God wants to connect with you. He wants you to know Him, come close to Him, hear His voice, and follow His lead.

> *How do you respond to the truth that you were created to know God in a deep and personal way?*

KNOW THE STORY

The following story is about two women who knew Jesus personally. Their names were Mary and Martha, and they were the sisters of a man named Lazarus. According to the Gospel of John, "Jesus loved Martha, her sister, and Lazarus" (John 11:5).

Jesus' love for Mary and Martha wasn't a general, unspecific love. It's true that God loves all people, but this was more. Jesus felt a genuine, human fondness for Mary, Martha, and their brother.

One day when Jesus was ministering and teaching near their community, He decided to stop off at His friends' house for dinner. Let's pick up the story there:

> [38] While they were traveling, he entered a village, and a woman named Martha welcomed him into her home. [39] She had a sister named Mary, who also sat at the Lord's feet and was listening to what he said. [40] But Martha was distracted by her many tasks, and she came up and asked, "Lord, don't you care that my sister has left me to serve alone? So tell her to give me a hand."
>
> [41] The Lord answered her, "Martha, Martha, you are worried and upset about many things, [42] but one thing is necessary. Mary has made the right choice, and it will not be taken away from her."
> LUKE 10:38-42

What do you find interesting from this story? Why?

What can we learn about Jesus from His interactions with Mary and Martha?

Both Mary and Martha were confronted with a choice between doing what felt necessary and spending time with Jesus. Don't miss the fact that Jesus decided which sister made the "right choice."

UNPACK THE STORY

TALK TO GOD THROUGH PRAYER

As a disciple of Jesus, you have an opportunity to spend time with Him each day. Therefore, like Mary and Martha, you need to make a choice. You can choose to dive headlong into the fast-moving current of your life with all its demands and frustrations—or you can choose to pull back and spend some time communicating with God.

You may be thinking, *How do I communicate with God?* Notice what Mary did to draw close to Jesus: she sat at His feet and listened to Him. That's it. That's all you need. Regularly drawing near to God and listening when He speaks to you are the keys to cultivating a deep and personal relationship with Him.

What are some potential obstacles that can hinder you from spending time with Jesus each day?

> Prayer isn't a way we get God to do what we want. Instead, prayer is the way we draw close to God to find out what He wants.

Prayer is one of the primary ways to talk with God and listen for His voice. People often feel confused about prayer—what it is, what it means, and what it accomplishes. At the core, however, prayer is simply communication with God. It involves speaking to God from your heart and actively listening when He speaks to you.

Notice that prayer isn't a method for approaching God as a genie or divine vending machine. Prayer isn't a way we get God to do what we want. Instead, prayer is the way we draw close to God to find out what He wants.

God draws us close to Himself when we spend time with Him in prayer. For that reason, saturating your life with prayer each day is the beginning step to knowing God and experiencing Him in a meaningful way.

What do you look forward to most when you think about prayer?

What questions would you like to ask about the process and purpose of prayer?

HEAR FROM GOD THROUGH HIS WORD

The more we draw close to God through prayer, the more open we become to hearing and receiving God's guidance in our lives. That's why the Bible is so important—because one of the primary ways God speaks to us today is through His Word.

When you read the Bible or hear teaching from the Scriptures, you are hearing from God. The Bible is unchanging, unwavering, unalterable, and always true. Though written thousands of years ago, it has remained both relevant and revolutionary literally for thousands of years.

In other words, the Bible is God's Word for you today!

What have you heard or been taught about the Bible?

What questions would you like to ask about God's Word?

The Scriptures offer clear principles and practical instructions for life. They are easily understood when studied seriously, and they are applicable for every disciple.

With that in mind, the most important tool you'll need for studying God's Word isn't a commentary or Bible dictionary—it's humility. Just as Mary submitted herself to Jesus by sitting at His feet, you must submit yourself to God's Word by choosing to believe and obey what it says.

When you read the Bible or hear teaching from the Scriptures, you are hearing from God.

As you hear from God through the pages of Scripture and begin to put His truth into practice, you'll continue to develop a deep love and close relationship with Him. In the same way that young children recognize their father's voice, you will begin to recognize and know your heavenly Father's voice as you study His Word.

What do you hope to experience as you study the Bible?

ENGAGE

Conclude this session by spending time praying together as a group. Use the acrostic PRAY as you follow the steps below. This method of prayer is based on the way Jesus taught His disciples to pray. (See pages 60-61 for a deeper exploration of the PRAY method.)

Note: groups with more than six participants may want to split into smaller subgroups so that everyone can participate.

- **Praise:** Begin by praising God. Acknowledge how He has worked for your benefit in recent weeks; express your desire to know Him and experience Him.

- **Repent:** Ask God to reveal any habits or life patterns that keep you from knowing Him more deeply. Confess the mistakes you've made and ask for God's forgiveness.

- **Ask:** Actively ask God to meet your needs and to draw you closer to Him in the coming week. Also pray for the others in your group.

- **Yield:** Conclude by yielding your whole self to God. Offer your life to Him this week, and affirm your desire to know Him and be used by Him.

PRAYER REQUESTS:

....

....

....

....

....

....

....

In addition to studying God's Word, work with your group leader to create a plan for personal study, worship, and application between now and the next session. Select from the following optional activities to match your personal preferences and available time.

↑ Worship

☑ Read your Bible. Complete the reading plan on page 56.

☐ Spend time with God by engaging the devotional experience on page 57.

☐ Connect with God each day. Select a time and place to spend time with God every day this week—preferably the same time and place in order to begin building a routine. In addition to reading God's Word (see the reading plan on the following page), pray about what you encounter.

➡ ⬅ Personal Study

☐ Read and interact with "How to Study the Bible" on page 58.

☐ Read and interact with "How to Pray" on page 60.

⬅ ➡ Application

☐ Connect with your church. Attend a church worship service and take notes as the pastor teaches from the Bible.

☐ Connect with others. Ask a friend or family member to join you this week in reading the Bible and connecting with God through prayer.

☐ Memorize John 10:14: "I am the good shepherd. I know my own, and my own know me."

☐ Express yourself. Respond to what you're learning from God and His Word by creating something—a painting, a poem, a song, etc.

☐ Other:

 # WORSHIP

READING PLAN

Continue reading through the Gospel of Mark this week. Use the space provided to record your thoughts and responses.

Day 1
Mark 9:14-32

Day 2
Mark 9:33-50

Day 3
Mark 10:1-16

Day 4
Mark 10:17-31

Day 5
Mark 10:32-52

Day 6
Mark 11:1-19

Day 7
Mark 11:20-33

INVESTING TIME

If you want to get to know someone better, you have to invest time with that person. The more time you spend together, the more you get to know each other and the deeper your relationship grows. Relationships require time in order to function well.

The same is true for your relationship with God. You were created to know Him in a deep and personal way, but doing so requires an investment on your end.

For that reason, set aside at least 30 minutes to spend with God—and only with God—within the next few days. Choose an environment that feels comfortable for you. This may be in your room with all your devices turned off, or it may be out in the woods with the sun on your face. Either way, intentionally limit this time to praying, studying God's Word, and actively listening for His guidance and direction.

When will I do this? _____

MY THOUGHTS:

HOW TO STUDY THE BIBLE

Along with prayer, reading the Bible is an essential element for disciples of Christ. The Bible is a miraculous work of literature that has changed the course of human history. It's actually a collection of 66 books written by 40 different authors over a period of more than 1,500 years—yet it tells a single, cohesive story about God and His work in the world. The Bible is the inspired Word of God entrusted to us as a precious gift. For these reasons and more, the Bible is worthy of our study and attention.

Maybe you're wondering: *How do I go about studying the Bible?* That's a good question, and we can begin finding answers in the Bible itself.

> **Read the following passages of Scripture and write down what they teach about saturating your life with God's Word.**
>
> **Psalm 119:9-16**

> **1 John 2:3-6**

One of the more difficult concepts to understand about the Bible is how different it is from other books. The Bible is not a spiritual textbook that provides information for living the way Christians are supposed to live. Therefore, reading the Bible should be more than merely an informational experience.

Instead, reading the Bible should be a transformational experience. The more you study God's Word, the more you should change and grow as a disciple of Jesus. That's what the Bible says:

> For the word of God is living and effective and sharper than any double-edged sword, penetrating as far as the separation of soul and spirit, joints and marrow. It is able to judge the thoughts and intentions of the heart.
> HEBREWS 4:12

> [16] All Scripture is inspired by God and is profitable for teaching, for rebuking, for correcting, for training in righteousness, [17] so that the man of God may be complete, equipped for every good work.
> 2 TIMOTHY 3:16-17

On a similar note, we need to recognize that the Bible was not written the same way other books are written. It's not the product of one person's imagination and experience. Rather, the Bible was written by men who were directly inspired by God's Holy Spirit:

> [20] Above all, you know this: No prophecy of Scripture comes from the prophet's own interpretation, [21] because no prophecy ever came by the will of man; instead, men spoke from God as they were carried along by the Holy Spirit.
> 2 PETER 1:20-21

In your own words, describe how the Bible is different from other books you've experienced.

For these reasons, one of the keys to studying the Bible is understanding from the beginning that the Bible is literally the Word of God—it's a supernatural book that ultimately comes from God, not from people.

Because of these realities, you should approach the Bible in a posture of humility and expectation. Use the following questions to help you focus on transformation and application as you study:

- What principles and truths does this text communicate?

- What commands and promises does this text contain?

- What are the implications of this text for my life today and in the days to come?

Finally, remember the words of Jesus as you seek to study His Word:

> [31] Then Jesus said to the Jews who had believed him, "If you continue in my word, you really are my disciples. [32] You will know the truth, and the truth will set you free."
> JOHN 8:31-32

How will you change your approach to studying the Bible based on what you've learned in this study?

HOW TO PRAY

You've seen that prayer is an essential practice for those who follow Jesus and want to connect with Him on a regular basis. In fact, prayer is the primary way Christians communicate with God. It's also one of the primary ways we hear Him speak back to us.

In other words, prayer is the foundation of our personal relationship with God.

But what does it mean to pray? And how do we actually go about the process of prayer? These aren't questions we should take lightly. Thankfully, we can learn from Jesus' example. While teaching His disciples how to pray, Jesus included a model prayer that includes the basic elements we should remember when communicating with God.

Take a look at Jesus' model prayer from the Gospel of Matthew:

> [9] "Therefore, you should pray like this:
> Our Father in heaven,
> your name be honored as holy.
> [10] Your kingdom come.
> Your will be done
> [11] on earth as it is in heaven.
> Give us today our daily bread.
> [12] And forgive us our debts,
> as we also have forgiven our debtors.
> [13] And do not bring us into temptation,
> but deliver us from the evil one."
> MATTHEW 6:9-13

What stands out to you about Jesus' example of how to pray?

How would you describe your experiences with prayer in the past?

You used the simple acrostic PRAY during the exercise on page 54. This is an easy way of remembering the different elements Jesus included in His model prayer.

- **P stands for praise.** Jesus began by praising his Father: "Our Father in heaven, your name be honored as holy" (v. 9). When you pray, don't rush into your requests and problems. First, praise God for who He is and recognize the positive ways He has worked in your life.

- **R stands for repent.** To repent means to turn from the direction you were going and follow Jesus, instead. Jesus prayed: "Your kingdom come. Your will be done on earth as it is in heaven" (vv. 10-11). Ask God to show you any area of your life where you've ignored or abandoned His will. Confess that to God and turn from it to follow Jesus wholeheartedly.

- **A stands for ask.** Jesus moved into asking for His daily needs in verses 11-13: "Give us … forgive us … deliver us" and more. When you pray, ask God to meet your needs and the needs of others.

- **Y stands for yield.** As you pray, it is an act of yielding your will before God. In prayer, we recognize God as our Father. He is the King of the kingdom. We ask for Him to be our Provider in both our physical and spiritual needs. Prayer is the place where we put our plans aside and ask God to lead us in every area of life.

It's also important to remember that prayer includes both talking and listening. Even as we open up to God about our thoughts, desires, and fears, we must also listen for His voice in answer. This kind of listening is intentional. It involves setting aside distractions—both internal and external—in order to actively hear what God chooses to speak to our hearts.

How confident do you feel in your ability to listen for God and hear His voice?

Spend a few moments in prayer using the PRAY method described above. How did it go?

THE BLESSING OF COMMUNITY

Following Jesus may be personal,
but it's never private.

REFLECT

In the previous session, we learned that all people are created to know God in a deep and personal way. This is a tremendous blessing we need to embrace whenever possible. As disciples of Jesus, we have the opportunity and responsibility to connect with God through prayer and through intentional encounters with His Word.

Which of the assignments did you explore this week? How did it go?

What did you learn or experience while reading the Bible?

What questions would you like to ask?

PRAY

Begin this session by connecting with God through prayer. Use the following guidelines as you speak with Him together:

- Thank God for the privilege of meeting together as part of a community.

- Talk to God honestly about your feelings and associations connected with the church, including your past experiences with church and church members.

- Ask for wisdom when it comes to finding your place and your voice in His community.

INTRODUCTION

In the movie *Cast Away*, Tom Hanks plays a likable guy named Chuck Noland whose airplane crashes into the Pacific Ocean at the beginning of the film. As the only survivor, Chuck spends the next four years on an uncharted island, isolated and alone.

Chuck's not friendless, however. He finds a volleyball tangled in some wreckage from the plane, draws a crude face on it, and names it Wilson. Then he begins to carry Wilson around the island with him. He engages Wilson in long conversations—even arguing with the ball over important decisions and life-threatening situations.

When Chuck finally builds a raft and attempts to escape the island's reef, he brings Wilson along. And when Wilson is ultimately lost at sea during Chuck's rescue, the man weeps uncontrollably at the "death" of his friend.

Chuck's story is fictional, but it's also a great illustration of an important truth: people were created to live in community.

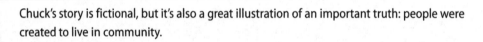

What emotions do you experience when you're alone for an extended period of time?

How do you respond to the truth that following Jesus was never intended to be a private relationship?

KNOW THE STORY

There are moments in human history that change everything. These extraordinary events mark the beginning of a new era, a new future, and even a new people. God chose to create such a moment 2,000 years ago when He launched the church. After Jesus' resurrection, He made this promise to His disciples:

> But you will receive power when the Holy Spirit has come on you, and you will be my witnesses in Jerusalem, in all Judea and Samaria, and to the end of the earth.
> ACTS 1:8

The fulfillment of that promise began weeks later. While Jesus' disciples were praying together, God's Holy Spirit came to them and filled each person with spiritual power. Inspired by this power, Peter proclaimed the message of the gospel to the people of Jerusalem. More than 3,000 people responded by choosing to follow Christ.

This was a major event in the life of the early church. And how did this new community of believers relate to one another? Check it out:

> [42] They devoted themselves to the apostles' teaching, to the fellowship, to the breaking of bread, and to prayer. [43] Everyone was filled with awe, and many wonders and signs were being performed through the apostles. [44] Now all the believers were together and held all things in common. [45] They sold their possessions and property and distributed the proceeds to all, as any had need. [46] Every day they devoted themselves to meeting together in the temple, and broke bread from house to house. They ate their food with joyful and sincere hearts, [47] praising God and enjoying the favor of all the people. Every day the Lord added to their number those who were being saved.
> ACTS 2:42-47

What do you find most interesting about these verses?

Circle the different ways the early church members engaged one another. Which of these excites you most? Why?

UNPACK THE STORY

WHAT IS THE CHURCH?

It's common in today's culture to associate the concept of "church" with a physical structure. When we think about church or about "going to church," we often see images of brick buildings, steeples, sanctuaries, parking lots, and so on.

It's also common for people to think of "church" as something that Christians do. We often make a connection between the church and the practices that are common in church buildings—sermons, worship songs, Sunday School, and more. Each of these associations is understandable, and each does point to the truth. Ultimately, the church involves much more.

What comes to mind when you hear the word "church"?

How would you describe your past experiences with church?

> The church is the community of people who follow Jesus Christ as Lord.

In reality, the church isn't a building or a collection of physical structures. Instead, the church is a collection of people. It's a community. In a similar way, the church isn't what we do, but who we are as followers of Jesus.

Here's a definition: the church is the community of people who follow Jesus Christ as Lord.

How do you respond to the above definition of church?

Every community comes together around specific actions and activities. A community of golfers joins together for the purpose of playing golf. A community of shoppers cruises the mall together, seeks out specific items for purchase, and enjoys sharing together about great deals and surprising finds.

The community of believers described in Acts 2 also shared common actions and activities. They gathered to learn about God by studying and discussing the Scriptures. They also gathered to serve God and support one another through the ups and downs of life by fellowshipping together, eating together, praying together, meeting one another's needs, and by making Jesus' love known to the world.

WHAT IS THE PURPOSE OF THE CHURCH?

There are two main purposes for the church:

1. To exist as a community of Christ-followers who support, encourage, and equip one another.
2. To serve as representatives of God's kingdom in order to accomplish His work in the world.

What do you look forward to when it comes to participating in the life of the church?

Both of these purposes are evident in Acts 2. Notice how the members of the church cared for one another: "They sold their possessions and property and distributed the proceeds to all, as any had need" (Acts 2:45).

Because of their love for one another, the earliest members of the church were willing to sacrifice their own possessions in order to meet the needs of others. Such selflessness didn't go unnoticed.

As the early Christians actively showed love to one another and proclaimed the message of the gospel, many outside the church became curious. They wanted to understand what had transformed Jesus' disciples into such caring and compassionate people. In the end, they realized Christ Himself was the source of that transformation. As a result, "every day the Lord added to their number those who were being saved" (Acts 2:47b).

Because of their love for one another, the earliest members of the church were willing to sacrifice their own possessions in order to meet the needs of others.

What emotions do you experience when you help others? Why?

When have you received encouragement or support as part of a community?

As a disciple of Jesus, there will be times when you find yourself in need of help. In those moments, you'll find support and encouragement within the community of believers—the church. There will also be times when others need your assistance, and you'll find great fulfillment in doing what's necessary to meet their needs as an expression of God's love.

ENGAGE

One of the main purposes of the church is to serve as a community in which disciples of Jesus can both give and receive support when needed. The church exists as a safe place for Christians to encourage and equip one another without fear of judgment or scorn—a place where our actions are guided not by selfishness, but by love.

That's the vision described by Jesus:

> [34] "I give you a new command: Love one another. Just as I have loved you, you are also to love one another. [35] By this everyone will know that you are my disciples, if you love one another."
> JOHN 13:34-35

The first step in giving or receiving support within the church is honest communication between church members. You can't offer prayer and practical support to fellow disciples of Jesus if you are unaware of their needs. Similarly, you won't receive prayer or practical support if you continually hold your struggles and challenges close to the vest.

Therefore, spend some time as a group discussing the following two questions. The goal of this exercise is not to force you to take on the responsibility of caring for other people. Instead, the goal is to practice sharing the deeper details of your life in order to highlight opportunities for mutual support.

When have you recently wished for help?

In what areas of life do you currently feel unsure or underprepared?

PRAYER REQUESTS:

....

....

....

....

....

In addition to studying God's Word, work with your group leader to create a plan for personal study, worship, and application between now and the next session. Select from the following optional activities to match your personal preferences and available time.

⬆ Worship

☑ Read your Bible. Complete the reading plan on page 70.

☐ Connect with God each day through prayer.

☐ Spend time with God by engaging the devotional experience on page 71.

➡⬅ Personal Study

☐ Read and interact with "Two Pictures of the Church" on page 72.

☐ Read and interact with "Two Practices of the Church" on page 74.

⬅➡ Application

☐ Become a church member. Speak with a pastor or staff person this week about the process and expectations involved with becoming an official member of your church.

☐ Memorize 1 Corinthians 12:27: "Now you are the body of Christ, and individual members of it."

☐ Invite a friend. As you experience the benefits of Christian community, describe those benefits to your friends and invite them along.

☐ Be social. Spend some "hang out" time with another member of your church or group during the week. Have lunch, chat over coffee, watch a movie, play a game—intentionally enjoy the privilege of being in community.

☐ Other:

 **WORSHIP**

READING PLAN

Continue reading through the Gospel of Mark this week. Use the space provided to record your thoughts and responses.

Day 1
Mark 12:1-17

Day 2
Mark 12:18-34

Day 3
Mark 12:35-44

Day 4
Mark 13:1-13

Day 5
Mark 13:14-37

Day 6
Mark 14:1-21

Day 7
Mark 14:22-31

WORSHIP ASSESSMENT

Worship is one of the great privileges of participating in the community known as the church. When we gather together as disciples of Jesus, we naturally join together in expressing our devotion to God and our appreciation for everything He has done. This is corporate worship.

For that reason, almost all church gatherings include an element of worship. For example, churches often participate in corporate worship through singing hymns and songs of praise to God. Many churches include additional elements such as visual arts, responsive reading, public testimony, corporate prayer, and more.

This week, take a step back as you participate in worship at your church. Examine yourself during the worship experience—keep track of your emotions and responses as you worship. Afterward, use the following questions to unpack your experience.

What did you appreciate most about your worship experience? Why?

What did you find confusing or unclear? Why?

How would you describe your efforts to connect with God during worship?

Where would you like to see improvement or greater depth in your efforts to worship God?

TWO PICTURES OF THE CHURCH

The authors of the Bible often used word pictures to help readers understand difficult or complicated concepts. Let's explore a few examples as we seek to understand the nature and purpose of the church.

First, the apostle Paul identified the church as the body of Christ:

> 12 For just as the body is one and has many parts, and all the parts of that body, though many, are one body—so also is Christ. 13 For we were all baptized by one Spirit into one body—whether Jews or Greeks, whether slaves or free—and we were all given one Spirit to drink. 14 Indeed, the body is not one part but many.
> 1 CORINTHIANS 12:12-14

What is your initial reaction to these verses?

Thinking of the church as a "body" is helpful in many ways. It reminds us that no part of the church is more important than the rest—although church leaders are responsible for guiding local churches and serving their members. On a large scale, Jesus Himself is the "head of the church" (Eph. 5:23). Jesus is the brain, and we are the body that exists to obey what He says and do what He wants.

Viewing the church as a "body" also teaches us that we need one another. We are a community of equals gathered into a body. To function well, we must work together. In fact, we must be unified even to the level of family and remember that God has brought us together according to His plan:

> 17 If the whole body were an eye, where would the hearing be? If the whole body were an ear, where would the sense of smell be? 18 But as it is, God has arranged each one of the parts in the body just as he wanted.
> 1 CORINTHIANS 12:17-18

How do these verses help you understand the nature of the church?

How do these verses help you understand your place in the church?

Second, the apostle Peter used several word pictures to describe the nature and purpose of the church:

> ⁹ But you are a chosen race, a royal priesthood, a holy nation, a people for his possession, so that you may proclaim the praises of the one who called you out of darkness into his marvelous light. ¹⁰ Once you were not a people, but now you are God's people; you had not received mercy, but now you have received mercy.
> 1 PETER 2:9-10

Circle the different concepts Peter used to describe the church.

As with 1 Corinthians, Peter's description of the church reminds us that followers of Jesus have been unified as a single community. It's true that Christians today are often subdivided into separate denominations or niches. We also gather together in local churches within our specific cities, suburbs, and towns. But at the core, we're all members of God's kingdom.

As members of the church, we are a distinct people group—a single spiritual nation spread throughout every political nation on earth.

This reality points to our purpose as the church. Because Christians are connected with one another as a "chosen race" and a "people," we are called to "proclaim the praises" of God (v. 9) and work together to accomplish His will for the world. We have "received mercy" as disciples of Jesus, and we have a responsibility to proclaim that message to others who are in need of mercy as well.

In other words, the blessing of joining together in community as disciples of Jesus should lead us to worship God and tell others about Him.

How do Peter's words help you understand the church's mission?

How do these verses help you understand your role in the church's mission?

TWO PRACTICES OF THE CHURCH

As members of the church, we have the opportunity to participate in a great range of activities intended to help us live and grow as followers of Jesus. These activities include worshiping God, hearing His Word preached, serving others, offering our resources, and so on. These are helpful activities that can benefit us in many ways as followers of Christ.

But let's focus on two specific church practices that help us remember who we are as a community of Christians. The first of those practices is baptism:

> ³ Or are you unaware that all of us who were baptized into Christ Jesus were baptized into his death? ⁴ Therefore we were buried with him by baptism into death, in order that, just as Christ was raised from the dead by the glory of the Father, so we too may walk in newness of life.
> ROMANS 6:3-4

What ideas or images come to mind when you hear the word "baptism"? Why?

The practice of baptism involves a new disciple of Jesus being immersed in water as a public declaration of faith in Christ. When the disciple is lowered into the water, it symbolizes his or her death to sin through the sacrifice of Jesus. And when the disciple is raised out of the water, it symbolizes his or her resurrection through Jesus as a new creation and a member of the church.

In other words, baptism is a public symbol and public declaration that a person has been "born again" as a follower of Jesus.

Read the following passages of Scripture and record what they teach about the practice and purpose of baptism:

Matthew 28:18-20

Acts 2:37-41

Acts 8:26-40

The second practice that reveals who we are as members of the church is called Communion—it's also referred to as "the Lord's Supper." Jesus Himself established this practice for the church during the Last Supper before His crucifixion:

> 19 And he took bread, gave thanks, broke it, gave it to them, and said, "This is my body, which is given for you. Do this in remembrance of me." 20 In the same way he also took the cup after supper and said, "This cup is the new covenant in my blood, which is poured out for you."
> LUKE 22:19-20

Different churches practice the Lord's Supper in different ways, but the basic elements are the same. Within the community of the church, disciples of Jesus obey His command by eating and drinking in order to remember His sacrifice on our behalf.

How would you describe your past experiences with the Lord's Supper?

What questions do you have about the practice of the Lord's Supper?

The practice of the Lord's Supper is vital because it reminds us of the nature of the church. Throughout the world and throughout the history of the church, disciples of Jesus have been linked together through the Lord's Supper. It helps unite us as a community.

In the same way, the Lord's Supper reminds us of the church's purpose. Even as we remember and commune with the death of Jesus as the payment for our sins, we're reminded that others need to experience His forgiveness. The Lord's Supper inspires us to share the gospel message with a world still in need of a Savior.

Now that you've learned about baptism and the Lord's Supper, what's your next step as a follower of Jesus?

JOINING JESUS ON MISSION

Disciples are called to know Christ, grow
with Christ, and go for Christ.

REFLECT

As we learned in the previous session, living as a disciple of Jesus is a deeply personal matter that must also be expressed in a public way. People are designed to live in community, which is why participation in the church—the community of people who follow Jesus Christ as Lord—is an essential part of following Jesus.

Which of the assignments did you explore this week? How did it go?

What did you learn or experience while reading the Bible?

What questions would you like to ask?

PRAY

Begin this session by connecting with God through prayer. Use the following guidelines as you speak with Him together:

- Thank God for creating the church and offering you the blessing of community.

- Ask God to give you an understanding of and a passion for His mission in the world.

- Ask for wisdom as you study what it means to join the church in working to achieve Christ's mission for the world.

INTRODUCTION

"Soldiers, Sailors and Airmen of the Allied Expeditionary Force! You are about to embark upon the Great Crusade, toward which we have striven these many months. The eyes of the world are upon you. The hopes and prayers of liberty-loving people everywhere march with you."[1]

These were the opening words of General Dwight D. Eisenhower when he sent the orders launching the D-Day invasion of June 6, 1944, near the end of World War II. Until that day, Axis forces held Europe in an iron grip of oppression and tyranny. The situation was grim. The world was waiting.

Thankfully, we know the rest of the story. The landing of Allied forces on the beaches of Normandy essentially turned the tide of the war. Less than a year later, the European campaign came to an end.

In a similar way, Jesus' life, death, and resurrection forever changed the course of human history. Although Jesus didn't use an army to achieve His victory over sin, He did launch the church—an ever-increasing, always-expanding movement of disciples.

As a follower of Christ, you're part of that movement. Therefore, you're called to participate in His continuing mission for the world. That mission contains several different elements, but they can all be boiled down to a core assignment: making disciples of Jesus Christ.

How do you feel about being included as a member of the movement called the church?

What emotions do you experience at the thought of telling others about Jesus?

KNOW THE STORY

Jesus talked often about His mission for the world. But His most memorable descriptions of that mission were connected with His first and last words to the disciples. The first came when He called the disciples to follow Him.

In Session 1 we explored this story from the perspective of choosing to follow Jesus. Now let's focus on Jesus' larger mission for the world:

> [18] As he was walking along the Sea of Galilee, he saw two brothers, Simon (who is called Peter), and his brother Andrew. They were casting a net into the sea—for they were fishermen. [19] "Follow me," he told them, "and I will make you fish for people." [20] Immediately they left their nets and followed him.
> MATTHEW 4:18-20

Jesus' mission for His disciples can be boiled down to two simple phrases: "Follow me" and "fish for people."

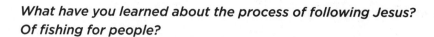

What have you learned about the process of following Jesus? Of fishing for people?

After His death and resurrection, Jesus confirmed and expanded His mission during one of His final conversations with the disciples:

> [18] Jesus came near and said to them, "All authority has been given to me in heaven and on earth. [19] Go, therefore, and make disciples of all nations, baptizing them in the name of the Father and of the Son and of the Holy Spirit, [20] teaching them to observe everything I have commanded you. And remember, I am with you always, to the end of the age."
> MATTHEW 28:18-20

How confident do you feel about obeying Jesus' commands in these verses? Why?

UNPACK THE STORY

YOUR MISSION IS FROM JESUS

Jesus' words from Matthew 28:18-20 are often referred to as the Great Commission. They summarize what Jesus commissioned, or sent, His disciples to do. And because Jesus extended the mission "to the end of the age" (v. 20), His words apply to all His disciples throughout history—including you.

As a new disciple of Christ, you are part of Jesus' continuing mission for the world. What's more, as a new disciple, you are called to participate in that mission by helping to make more disciples of Christ.

What emotions do you experience when you think about "making disciples" of Jesus? Why?

> As a new disciple of Christ, you are part of Jesus' continuing mission for the world.

With that in mind, remember that the foundation of Jesus' commission was His own authority. Jesus said: "All authority has been given to me in heaven and on earth" (v. 18). In other words, He wanted everyone to understand that He's in charge of everything connected to this world—and beyond.

Why is that important? Because a mission is only as good as the person (or Person) commanding it.

If a regular soldier had sent out the order to attack on D-Day, nobody would have paid attention. But since the orders came instead from the general in command, they had weight. They carried authority that demanded obedience.

In the same way, Jesus is the most important person who ever lived. His life, death, and resurrection are the central moments in human history, and He exists as both God and man. Therefore, His words demand obedience from us.

How do you respond to Jesus' claim of authority?

YOUR MISSION IS TO MAKE DISCIPLES

The core of Jesus' statement from the Great Commission is "make disciples of all nations" (v. 19). But how do we do that? What does it look like to make disciples? Where do we get started, and what are we supposed to do?

Fortunately, Jesus offered three practical steps we can follow in order to make new disciples in His Name:

- **Go:** You can't be passive about making disciples. Jesus commanded us to go to our family members, go to our friends, go into our communities, and even go throughout the world as we proclaim the gospel.

- **Baptize:** To be baptized is to make a public declaration of faith in Jesus Christ. This helps us remember our mission isn't to get people to stop sinning, or even to convince them to attend church. Our mission is to proclaim the good news of Jesus Christ and help others confess Him as Lord.

- **Teach:** The process of making a disciple doesn't end at conversion. When someone experiences salvation, we're called to teach them to observe everything Jesus commanded. In other words, we have a responsibility to teach new disciples what it means to live as a disciple of Christ.

Which of the above steps seems most difficult to you? Why?

How have you experienced the process of discipleship in your journey as a follower of Christ?

You will never be finished as a disciple of Jesus. You will always have room to grow and mature.

The process of making disciples for Jesus is called discipleship. And it is a process—it takes time. In fact, you will never be finished as a disciple of Jesus. You will always have room to grow and mature.

Therefore, be patient with yourself. And be patient with the people you serve as you begin the ministry of making disciples.

ENGAGE

Taking advantage of opportunities to share your testimony—your story of experiencing salvation and choosing to follow Jesus—will be one of your most effective tools for making disciples. Many Christians feel nervous at the thought of sharing their testimony, but doing so doesn't have to be a frightening or frustrating experience. Nor does it need to be confrontational.

Instead, simply talk through your answers to the following questions:

How would you describe your life before you encountered Jesus?

How did you come to know and follow Jesus?

What changes have you experienced since becoming a disciple of Jesus?

Telling your story can be a powerful experience—both for you and for those who hear you. As time allows, practice sharing your testimony with the members of your group. Use this experience to gain insight and feedback so you can be ready when the time comes for you to share the good news of salvation with someone who needs to hear it.

PRAYER REQUESTS:

....

....

....

....

....

....

....

....

1. Jonathan Foreman, *The Pocket Book of Patriotism* (New York: Sterling Publishing Co. Inc., 2005), 75.

In addition to studying God's Word, work with your group leader to create a plan for personal study, worship, and application between now and the next session. Select from the following optional activities to match your personal preferences and available time.

⬆ Worship

☑ Read your Bible. Complete the reading plan on page 84.

☐ Connect with God by praying about your place in His mission for the world. Ask God to show you opportunities to help make disciples each day.

☐ Spend time with God by engaging the devotional experience on page 85.

➡⬅ Personal Study

☐ Read and interact with "Your Mission Is for the World" on page 86.

☐ Read and interact with "Your Mission Includes the Church" on page 88.

⬅➡ Application

☐ Go for it. Share your testimony this week with at least one person who needs to experience what Jesus has to offer.

☐ Memorize John 14:6: "Jesus told him, 'I am the way, the truth, and the life. No one comes to the Father except through me.'"

☐ Look to your community. Meet with your pastor or a church staff member to determine specific ways you can spread the message of the gospel within your local community.

☐ Look to the ends of the earth. Research individuals and organizations currently working to spread the gospel internationally. Determine a way you can participate in that ministry throughout the week.

☐ Other:

 **WORSHIP**

READING PLAN

Continue reading through the Gospel of Mark this week. Use the space provided to record your thoughts and responses.

Day 1
Mark 14:32-52

Day 2
Mark 14:53-72

Day 3
Mark 15:1-15

Day 4
Mark 15:16-32

Day 5
Mark 15:33-47

Day 6
Mark 16:1-8

Day 7
Mark 16:9-20

PRAYER MISSION

Here's another time when Jesus spoke with His disciples about their mission in the world:

> [1] After this, the Lord appointed seventy-two others, and he sent them ahead of him in pairs to every town and place where he himself was about to go. [2] He told them, "The harvest is abundant, but the workers are few. Therefore, pray to the Lord of the harvest to send out workers into his harvest."
> LUKE 10:1-2

You must not forget to pray as you seek to obey Jesus' mission of making disciples. In fact, prayer is one of your most valuable and effective resources in that mission.

For that reason, spend some time making a list of the different people in your life who need to hear the message of the gospel and experience salvation. Think of as many people as you can. As you write each name, pray that God would make Himself known to that person, and that he or she would experience salvation through Jesus Christ.

MY LIST:

YOUR MISSION IS FOR THE WORLD

The four Gospels at the beginning of the New Testament all tell the story of Jesus. The Book of Acts describes the birth and early stages of the church. For that reason, it's important to understand that Jesus Himself launched the church by stating once again His mission for any who choose to follow Him:

> ⁷ He said to them, "It is not for you to know times or periods that the Father has set by his own authority. ⁸ But you will receive power when the Holy Spirit has come on you, and you will be my witnesses in Jerusalem, in all Judea and Samaria, and to the end of the earth." ⁹ After he had said this, he was taken up as they were watching, and a cloud took him out of their sight.
> ACTS 1:7-9

How do these verses connect with the Great Commission? (See page 80.)

Notice that Jesus mentioned three specific places in which His disciples will serve as witnesses: in Jerusalem, in all Judea and Samaria, and to the end of the earth. Looking more deeply at these locations will help us carry out our mission as followers of Christ.

First, Jerusalem was essentially home for Jesus' first disciples. As the major city in Israel, it represented everything that was familiar and comfortable to the disciples. They had grown up around Jerusalem, they had ministered with Jesus in Jerusalem, and they would spend most of their time in Jerusalem after Jesus ascended into heaven (see Acts 1:4).

As a modern disciple of Jesus, you're also called to serve in your version of "Jerusalem." In other words, your first actions as a witness for Jesus should be centered around your home—around the places where you feel most comfortable. You're called to speak with your family members and closest friends about your decision to follow Christ.

What questions do you have about talking to your family members and closest friends about Jesus?

What steps can you take to begin sharing the gospel with the people you care about?

Second, the phrase "all Judea and Samaria" referred to the broader regions around Jerusalem. These were the homes of people from different races and nationalities—people who were considered outsiders or even enemies by the Jews. Jesus commissioned His first disciples to reach out to people not like themselves.

In the same way, you're called to serve the people in your community who are different from you. You're called to be a witness for Jesus in your workplace, in your neighborhood, in your interactions with acquaintances, and even in your encounters with strangers.

What's your initial reaction to the above statements?

What steps can you take to intentionally serve as a witness for Jesus in your neighborhood and community?

Third, Jesus commanded His disciples to be witnesses "to the end of the earth." Amazingly, they obeyed. Jesus' original disciples were the founders of the church. Through their efforts, the church grew at an incredible rate and has continued to expand for centuries—bringing the message of Jesus to every corner of the world.

As a disciple of Jesus, you are part of that church. Therefore, you have inherited the continued mission to spread the gospel message to the end of the earth. That doesn't mean you're obligated to become a missionary, but it does mean you have been called to play a part in proclaiming the gospel throughout all nations.

What questions do you have about serving as a witness for Jesus even "to the end of the earth"?

What steps can you take to begin obeying Jesus' commands?

➡️⬅️ PERSONAL STUDY

YOUR MISSION INCLUDES THE CHURCH

As a disciple of Jesus, you've inherited His commission to "make disciples of all nations" (Matt. 28:19). You've also been given His command to serve as His witness "in Jerusalem, and in all Judea and Samaria, and to the end of the earth" (Acts 1:8). Obviously, you can't fulfill either of those charges by yourself. You need to be part of something bigger—something capable of reaching through your community and outward to the entire world.

In other words, you need the church in order to fulfill your mission as a disciple of Christ.

How do you respond to the above statement?

As we saw in session 5, the church is the community of people who follow Jesus as Lord. We don't follow Him only as individuals, however. We are connected together as the body of Christ. We all have specific roles within that body, and we've all been given gifts—often referred to as "spiritual gifts"— to help us engage our mission effectively:

> ⁴ Now as we have many parts in one body, and all the parts do not have the same function, ⁵ in the same way we who are many are one body in Christ and individually members of one another. ⁶ According to the grace given to us, we have different gifts: If prophecy, use it according to the proportion of one's faith; ⁷ if service, use it in service; if teaching, in teaching; ⁸ if exhorting, in exhortation; giving, with generosity; leading, with diligence; showing mercy, with cheerfulness.
> ROMANS 12:4-8

What are some gifts, talents, or abilities you've been given as a follower of Jesus?

What steps can you take to use those gifts as a member of the church?

The important thing to remember about spiritual gifts is that every follower of Jesus is unique and uniquely gifted to serve Him—including you. It's also important to understand that the church is most healthy when all of Jesus' disciples do their parts to carry out His mission.

That's a point the apostle Paul made in the Book of Ephesians:

> 15 But speaking the truth in love, let us grow in every way into him who is the head—Christ. 16 From him the whole body, fitted and knit together by every supporting ligament, promotes the growth of the body for building up itself in love by the proper working of each individual part.
> EPHESIANS 4:15-16

There's a progression involved in the working of the church. Jesus is Head of the body of Christ. When we stay connected to Him as His disciples, we remain spiritually healthy. And when we use our gifts to participate in the church and fulfill the commission He has given us, the church remains healthy.

And as we've seen many times throughout history, a healthy church can change the world in miraculous ways.

How have you seen the church bless your community?

How have you seen the church bless the world?

God's will for your life is that you come to know Jesus in a deep and personal way, that you grow in your relationship with Him, and that you use your gifts to advance His mission for the world through the community of the church.

What are some next steps you will take in order to continue advancing as a disciple of Jesus?

DEFINING
A DISCIPLE

To be a disciple of Jesus is to participate in
God's redemptive mission for the world.

REFLECT

In the previous session we unpacked the first and last words Jesus had with His disciples. As you continue to explore the process of growing and maturing as a disciple of Jesus, don't miss the responsibility every believer shares to make Jesus famous in the world.

Before we continue to examine the journey of Jesus' own disciples through different passages from the Gospels, let's first reflect on the topic from the previous week.

Which of the assignments did you explore this week? How did it go?

What did you learn or experience while reading the Bible?

What questions would you like to ask?

PRAY

Begin this session by connecting with God through prayer. Use the following guidelines as you speak with Him together:

- Thank God for the opportunity to join with other disciples of Christ in order to gain a better understanding of what it means to live as a disciple.

- Praise God for the ways He has worked in your life.

- Ask for wisdom for all present as you engage God's Word.

INTRODUCTION

The English language has a lot of quirks. There are bunches of rules and principles that are supposed to keep things separated and in order. Yet many times those rules and principles overlap in strange ways—even sometimes contradicting one another.

For example, did you know many English words can be used as both nouns and verbs? Think of a farmer milking a cow. The word *milk* acts as a verb in such situations; to "milk" a cow is an action that involves specific steps. But what do you get after the cow has been milked? You get milk, of course—*milk* as a noun. The same word goes in two separate directions.

Other words follow the same pattern. You might smell (verb) something wonderful in your kitchen and recognize it as the smell (noun) of baking bread. You can use a hammer (noun) to hammer (verb) nails into a board. Strange as it may sound, it's entirely possible to chant a chant, broadcast a broadcast, and drink a drink.

Disciple is another word that can go in two directions at once. Those who have experienced salvation live and breathe each day as disciples of Jesus Christ. In this way, the word *disciple* defines who we are as Christians. At the same time, the term also defines much of what we do as Christians. As followers of Jesus, we're called to disciple less-mature Christians by helping them grow in their relationships with Christ—even as we are discipled by others.

This process is called "discipleship," and it's one of the primary goals of this session. As you have begun to engage the pages to come, you'll learn what it means to find your identity as a disciple of Jesus. You'll also learn (and experience) the benefits of discipleship in the context of deeper relationships with other Christians.

How would you summarize in your own words what it means to be a disciple of Jesus Christ?

What questions do you have about the meaning and process of discipleship?

KNOW THE STORY

John the Baptist was a man with a mission. He had been charged by God to prepare the way for the Messiah—for Jesus. The following story highlights Jesus' mission for the world. It also helps us gain a sense of our place in that mission as disciples of Christ.

29 The next day John saw Jesus coming toward him and said, "Here is the Lamb of God, who takes away the sin of the world! 30 This is the one I told you about: 'After me comes a man who ranks ahead of me, because he existed before me.' 31 I didn't know him, but I came baptizing with water so he might be revealed to Israel."

32 And John testified, "I saw the Spirit descending from heaven like a dove, and he rested on him. 33 I didn't know him, but he who sent me to baptize with water told me, 'The one you see the Spirit descending and resting on—he is the one who baptizes with the Holy Spirit.' 34 I have seen and testified that this is the Son of God."

35 The next day, John was standing with two of his disciples. 36 When he saw Jesus passing by, he said, "Look, the Lamb of God!" 37 The two disciples heard him say this and followed Jesus. 38 When Jesus turned and noticed them following him, he asked them, "What are you looking for?" They said to him, "Rabbi" (which means "Teacher"), "where are you staying?" 39 "Come and you'll see," he replied. So they went and saw where he was staying, and they stayed with him that day. It was about four in the afternoon.

40 Andrew, Simon Peter's brother, was one of the two who heard John and followed him. 41 He first found his own brother Simon and told him, "We have found the Messiah" (which is translated "the Christ"), 42 and he brought Simon to Jesus.
JOHN 1:29-42

What do these verses teach us about Jesus?

UNPACK THE STORY

JESUS HAS A MISSION FOR THE WORLD

We're exploring the question: *What does it mean to be a disciple of Jesus?* Interestingly, the best way to answer that question is to focus not on the concept of a "disciple," but on the identity of Jesus. In order to understand what it means to live as followers of Jesus, we must first have a proper view of Jesus Himself.

What are some different ways people define Jesus today?

How would you express or explain who Jesus is?

> Jesus came to fix the problem of sin. His death and resurrection opened the door for redemption— they allow us to experience forgiveness for our sins and live in a restored (or redeemed) relationship with God. This is the gospel.

John the Baptist offered several identifying factors for Jesus. For example, John claimed that Jesus existed before him, even though John was older than Jesus by several months (see Luke 1). More importantly, John identified Jesus as "the Lamb of God," "the Son of God," and "the one who baptizes with the Holy Spirit."

All of these factors point to a vital truth: Jesus is more than a regular person. In fact, Jesus is God in human flesh. One of the foundational concepts of Christianity is the doctrine of the incarnation, which states that Jesus is both fully God and fully human. Jesus' time on earth involved the fullness of God interacting with humanity and all of creation both physically and historically.

Jesus didn't come to earth for a vacation, however. He had a purpose. He had a mission. And it was this mission John the Baptist referenced when he saw Jesus for the first time: "Here is the Lamb of God, who takes away the sin of the world!" (John 1:29).

The world has been broken and corrupted by sin. We as individuals are broken and corrupted by sin. But Jesus came to fix the problem of sin. His death and resurrection opened the door for redemption—they allow us to experience forgiveness for our sins and live in a restored (or redeemed) relationship with God. This is the gospel.

Where have you seen evidence of Jesus' mission?

DISCIPLES PARTICIPATE IN JESUS' MISSION FOR THE WORLD

To live as disciples of Jesus, we must first understand His redemptive mission for the world. As with most things, however, it's not enough for us to simply *understand* Jesus' redemptive mission for the world. We must go further. We must take action. Indeed, to be a disciple of Jesus is to *participate* in His mission and purpose for the world.

Notice from our Scripture focus that John the Baptist wasn't content with recognizing Jesus as "the Lamb of God." John took pains to publicly proclaim the truth about Jesus on multiple occasions. He took action in order to participate in Jesus' mission and purpose. And his participation produced fruit—men who had been following John were rightly convinced to follow Jesus, instead (see vv. 37-39).

In a similar way, verse 40 shows how Andrew—one of the two men who had been following John—participated in Jesus' mission by sharing the good news with his brother, Simon. Andrew's efforts went beyond words. He brought Simon to Jesus so that his brother could experience the truth for himself.

How would you describe your experiences of talking with others about Jesus?

In addition to evangelism, what are some other ways we can participate in Jesus' mission for the world?

As you read through Scripture—and as you continue working through the pages of this resource—you'll notice that Jesus' disciples rarely engage His mission as individuals. Instead, followers of Christ typically work together in relationship with one another as they seek to advance His redemptive mission in the world. That was certainly Jesus' preference during His public ministry. He didn't recruit converts and then send them out to do His work in isolation. Instead, He gathered disciples to Himself so they could follow Him as a community—even as a family.

What are some advantages of working as a team to engage Jesus' mission for the world?

Jesus' disciples rarely engage His mission as individuals. Instead, followers of Christ typically work together in relationship with one another as they seek to advance His redemptive mission in the world.

ENGAGE

Following Jesus is not an individual activity, nor is it something that can be accomplished in isolation— not for long. Instead, living as a disciple of Christ means living within a community of Christians. That community extends around the world and throughout time to include the church in all ages and all locations. On a more practical level, however, your local community includes the fellow disciples you connect with, worship with, and serve with each week.

Take a few minutes to practice living as a community of disciples in the following two ways:

1. Pray with one another. Spend several minutes praying together as a group. Talk openly about the major events in your life, including both difficulties and triumphs. Then take turns praying for one another specifically and intentionally.

2. Connect with one another. Plan a time to meet socially as a group and do something fun, preferably before the next group meeting. Meet at a park, have dinner, watch a movie—anything that moves you forward together in community.

PRAYER REQUESTS

....

....

....

....

....

....

....

....

....

....

....

....

In addition to studying God's Word, work with your group leader to create a plan for personal study, worship, and application between now and the next session. Select from the following optional activities to match your personal preferences and available time.

⬆ Worship

☑ Read your Bible. Complete the reading plan on page 98.

☐ Spend time with God by engaging the devotional experience on page 99.

☐ Connect with God each day through prayer.

➡ ⬅ Personal Study

☐ Read and interact with "Jesus Has a Mission for the World" on page 100.

☐ Read and interact with "Disciples Participate in Jesus' Mission" on page 102.

⬅ ➡ Application

☐ Be intentional about making the most of your experiences at church this weekend. Take advantage of opportunities to engage other disciples of Jesus in a more meaningful way.

☐ Memorize John 1:29: "The next day John saw Jesus coming toward him and said, 'Here is the Lamb of God, who takes away the sin of the world!'"

☐ When you have an opportunity to participate in Jesus' mission this week, invite another disciple to join you.

☐ Start a journal to record the different ways you engage Jesus' mission for the world each day. This is a great way to remind yourself of that mission and evaluate your participation in it.

☐ Other:

WORSHIP

READING PLAN

Read through the following Scripture passages this week. Use the space provided to record your thoughts and responses.

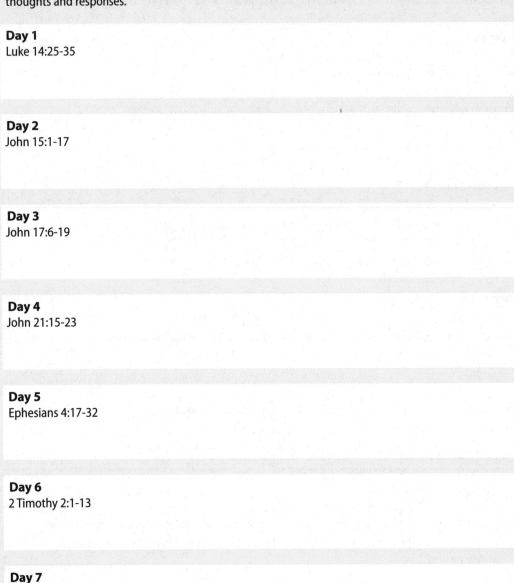

Day 1
Luke 14:25-35

Day 2
John 15:1-17

Day 3
John 17:6-19

Day 4
John 21:15-23

Day 5
Ephesians 4:17-32

Day 6
2 Timothy 2:1-13

Day 7
2 Timothy 2:14-26

TO SERVE AND TO GIVE

As you'd expect, Jesus' earliest disciples had a lot of learning to do about what it meant to follow Him. For example, they spent much of their time in a strange kind of sibling rivalry—they pushed and jockeyed with one another in order to see who would become the greatest in Jesus' kingdom. The disciples knew Jesus was something special and they understood Him to be both majestic and powerful. Therefore, each wanted to position himself to receive the largest portion of reflected majesty and power once Jesus declared Himself to the world as King.

Of course, none of that was in Jesus' plans. And He let them know it:

> 42 Jesus called them over and said to them, "You know that those who are regarded as rulers of the Gentiles lord it over them and those in high positions act as tyrants over them. 43 But it is not so among you. On the contrary, whoever wants to become great among you will be your servant, 44 and whoever wants to be first among you will be a slave to all. 45 For even the Son of Man did not come to be served, but to serve, and to give his life as a ransom for many."
> MARK 10:42-45

We must also be careful of pride and ambition as we seek to follow Jesus—mainly because such attitudes will damage our relationship with Him. Use the following questions to assess your heart.

What factors cause you to feel jealous of or competitive with other disciples?

In what situations do you feel superior to other people? Why?

How do you feel when you intentionally work for the benefit of others?

Following Jesus isn't about notoriety and big rewards—not in this life, anyway. Instead, those who choose to live as disciples of Christ must constantly give of themselves in order to serve others, as He did.

PERSONAL STUDY

JESUS HAS A MISSION FOR THE WORLD

What does it mean to be a disciple of Jesus? At the core, it means to join with other disciples in order to participate in His broader mission for the world. To that end, we've already seen that Jesus' mission centers on His role as the One "who takes away the sin of the world" (John 1:29). But let's dig a little deeper into that mission—and into the identify of Jesus Himself—in order to better understand what's expected of us as disciples.

John the Baptist provides an interesting character study for these themes. While he spent his life preparing the way for the Messiah, he didn't encounter Jesus until the end of his ministry. Yet, we can learn much from John when it comes to living in light of Jesus' person and mission.

Look at the following passage, for example:

> ¹⁵ Now the people were waiting expectantly, and all of them were questioning in their hearts whether John might be the Messiah. ¹⁶ John answered them all, "I baptize you with water, but one who is more powerful than I am is coming. I am not worthy to untie the strap of his sandals. He will baptize you with the Holy Spirit and fire. ¹⁷ His winnowing shovel is in his hand to clear his threshing floor and gather the wheat into his barn, but the chaff he will burn with fire that never goes out."
> LUKE 3:15-17

What can we learn about John the Baptist from these verses?

What can we learn about Jesus from these verses?

The people of John's day were looking for the Messiah, a specific term for the Savior of the world prophesied throughout the Old Testament. John knew the Messiah would be Someone greater than himself—Someone with the power to both save people for eternity ("gather the wheat into his barn") and pronounce judgment for sin ("the chaff he will burn with fire").

In addition, John understood that the Messiah would grant people access to God's Spirit. John baptized people with water as a symbol. The Messiah would baptize "with the Holy Spirit and fire."

All of this is important because it helps us understand that Jesus' mission for the world is directly connected to His divine authority and divine identity. The reason Jesus can fix the brokenness of the world is because He created the world. The reason Jesus can provide forgiveness for sin is because He is God; therefore, He is totally untouched by sin. For these reasons and more, we can feel confident as participants in Jesus' mission.

In order to live as disciples of Jesus, we must first fully embrace His identity as God. Thankfully, Jesus made His identity clear throughout the Scriptures, including here:

> 27 My sheep hear my voice, I know them, and they follow me. 28 I give them eternal life, and they will never perish. No one will snatch them out of my hand. 29 My Father, who has given them to me, is greater than all. No one is able to snatch them out of the Father's hand. 30 I and the Father are one."
> JOHN 10:27-30

How did you come to the conclusion that Jesus is God?

In a similar way, Jesus wasn't silent about the nature of His mission for the world. He spoke often of His purpose and His goals as Savior.

Read the following passages of Scripture and record how they contribute to your understanding of Jesus' mission for the world:

Mark 10:42-45

Luke 4:16-21

John 17:1-5

Living as a disciple of Jesus means embracing His identity and His mission for the world. Be sure you've taken that crucial step as you consider what it means to follow Him each day.

DISCIPLES PARTICIPATE IN JESUS' MISSION

In order to live as disciples of Jesus, we must fully embrace His mission as the divine Savior of the world. But that's just the first step. In addition to understanding and embracing Jesus' mission for the world, we must also participate in that mission. We need to get involved.

But what does that mean on a practical level? How do we actually go about joining Jesus in His redemptive purpose for the world? We'll spend the remainder of this resource exploring answers to those questions. Specifically, we'll focus on four ways Jesus empowers those who follow Him:

1. Jesus calls His disciples.
2. Jesus teaches His disciples.
3. Jesus equips His disciples.
4. Jesus sends His disciples.

Which item from this list are you most interested in exploring? Why?

Before we move forward, however, let's look at two important truths that will help us gain a deeper understanding of what it means to participate in Jesus' mission for the world. First, our involvement in Jesus' mission goes beyond "participation" in the normal sense of that word. We don't participate with Jesus in the same way we participate in the Parent Teacher Association or a charitable cause—we don't "pitch in" with Jesus' mission whenever our schedule opens up.

No, to follow Jesus means to give up our lives in service to Him. Jesus Himself made that clear:

> 23 Then he said to them all, "If anyone wants to follow after me, let him deny himself, take up his cross daily, and follow me. 24 For whoever wants to save his life will lose it, but whoever loses his life because of me will save it."
> LUKE 9:23-24

What's your initial reaction to these verses?

Jesus wasn't necessarily talking about physically dying for His mission—although many of His followers have done so over the centuries. Instead, Jesus wanted us to understand that joining His purpose for the world means giving over control of our lives to Him. Following Jesus means we not only recognize Him as Savior, but also submit to Him as Master, Lord, and King.

In what ways have you already submitted yourself to Jesus?

What steps can you take in the coming weeks to continue releasing control of your life over to Him?

Second, we need to understand that our involvement in Jesus' mission depends on His strength and resources rather than our own. It's easy for Christians to get the wrong idea on this subject—it's easy for us to feel like the world is on our shoulders and all of God's plans will collapse if we don't pray harder, worship longer, read the Bible more frequently, and evangelize until we drop.

Thankfully, Jesus again made things clear in His Word:

> I am the vine; you are the branches. The one who remains in me and I in him produces much fruit, because you can do nothing without me.
> JOHN 15:5

How have you benefited from Jesus' presence and power in your life?

What kinds of fruit do you hope will be produced in your life as a disciple of Jesus?

As a disciple of Jesus, you will participate in His mission when you submit control of your life to Him and actively rely on His resources to work through you and produce fruit.

DEFINING DISCIPLESHIP

To live as a disciple of Jesus includes
embracing a lifestyle of discipleship.

REFLECT

We established in the previous session that disciples of Jesus are those who actively participate in His mission for the world. This participation is a far cry from the passive, purpose-less lifestyle of those who embrace a culture of Christianity without actually obeying the will of Christ. As we continue in this session, we'll see that participating in Jesus' mission for the world as His disciples also means choosing to engage a lifestyle of discipleship.

As you prepare to explore part of Paul's letter to Timothy, take a moment to reflect on your experiences in recent days.

Which of the assignments did you explore this week? How did it go?

What did you learn or experience while reading the Bible?

What questions would you like to ask?

PRAY

Begin this session by connecting with God through prayer. Use the following guidelines as you speak with Him together:

- Praise God for providing each of His disciples with the privilege of participating in the critical ministry of discipleship.

- Thank God for the blessing of community as you seek to obey His will together.

- Pray that God would bless the members of your group with the gift of conviction—that He would alert you through His Spirit when you wander away from His will.

INTRODUCTION

Did you know that animal hybrids actually exist? True, you can't find the wild combinations that were common in ancient mythologies, such as the Griffin or the Centaur. But there are real, living animals in the world today that represent the combination of two distinct species.

The mule is the most common of these hybrids. Part horse and part donkey, mules have been valued in many regions and civilizations over the centuries because of their strength and versatility. Pound for pound, mules are stronger than horses and as intelligent as donkeys—and they don't even eat very much!

Other, stranger animal hybrids can be found in the wild. For example, travelers in the Northwest Territories of Canada have, on multiple occasions, come across a terrifying creature known as the Grolar Bear. That would be a half Grizzly, half Polar Bear. Scientists have also confirmed the existence of a Wholphin—an animal that is half whale and half dolphin.

What kinds of animals piqued your curiosity as a child?

When have you encountered an especially interesting creature?

Although these creatures may be interesting, it's important to remember that hybrid animals cannot replicate themselves. Neither Grolar Bears nor Wholphins possess the necessary genetic material to reproduce; they are sterile. A mule can never be a parent.

This fact reminds us that reproduction is a critical process in the natural world. Animal species will only thrive and grow within their environments when they are successful at reproducing themselves from generation to generation.

The same is true with followers of Christ. We've seen that disciples of Jesus must participate in His mission for the world in order to be spiritually healthy. At the same time, disciples must participate in the ongoing process of discipleship in order for the church to grow and thrive in its natural environment.

KNOW THE STORY

The inaugural years of the church were an exciting and confusing time for the earliest disciples of Jesus. They were exciting because of the many ways in which God's Spirit moved to accomplish mighty things. They were sometimes confusing because the earliest disciples were still figuring out what it meant to live as followers of Christ in their everyday lives.

That's why the epistles were so important. These letters helped clarify important elements of the Christian life, including the importance of discipleship. That's the focus of the following words written by the apostle Paul to Timothy, his spiritual son:

> [1] You, therefore, my son, be strong in the grace that is in Christ Jesus. [2] What you have heard from me in the presence of many witnesses, commit to faithful men who will be able to teach others also.
>
> [3] Share in suffering as a good soldier of Christ Jesus. [4] No one serving as a soldier gets entangled in the concerns of civilian life; he seeks to please the commanding officer. [5] Also, if anyone competes as an athlete, he is not crowned unless he competes according to the rules. [6] The hardworking farmer ought to be the first to get a share of the crops. [7] Consider what I say, for the Lord will give you understanding in everything.
>
> [8] Remember Jesus Christ, risen from the dead and descended from David, according to my gospel, [9] for which I suffer to the point of being bound like a criminal. But the word of God is not bound. [10] This is why I endure all things for the elect: so that they also may obtain salvation, which is in Christ Jesus, with eternal glory.
> 2 TIMOTHY 2:1-10

What are some keys to the Christian life in these verses?

Which of Paul's commands in the above passage are especially applicable in your life right now?

UNPACK THE STORY

DISCIPLESHIP IS A PROCESS

There is no set definition for the term "discipleship" within the church. But for our purposes, we'll define discipleship as the process of growing toward maturity as a follower of Jesus—and helping others do the same.

Don't overlook that word "process." It's important. Receiving the gift of salvation is the beginning of your journey as a disciple of Jesus, but it's a journey that will require the rest of your life. Your growth as a Christian and your work to help others grow spiritually is a process that will take time—and one that will require both grace and endurance.

> ¹ You, therefore, my son, be strong in the grace that is in Christ Jesus. ² What you have heard from me in the presence of many witnesses, commit to faithful men who will be able to teach others also.
> 2 TIMOTHY 2:1-2

Discipleship is the process of growing toward maturity as a follower of Jesus—and helping others do the same.

What do Paul's words communicate about the process of discipleship?

Look again at verses 1-10. How should we understand Paul's repeated calls for strength, faithfulness, and endurance?

Paul's instructions in verse 2 are also an important reminder that discipleship is not only a process for individuals, but for larger groups of disciples within the church. At the time he wrote this letter, Paul had already invested years into helping Timothy develop as a leader in the church. Now, Paul reminded Timothy of his obligation to train and develop other "faithful men" within the community—and to train them in such a way that they would "be able to teach others also."

In other words, we must think of discipleship in terms of spiritual generations.

How would you describe your walk with Christ in terms of spiritual generations?

DISCIPLESHIP IS PURPOSEFUL

Another key truth emphasized by Paul is the fact that discipleship is an intentional process. It's purposeful. A child's body will grow physically as long as it's provided with a minimum amount of food, water, and rest. Therefore, children don't have to be intentional about progressing toward physical maturity; it's an automated process.

Spiritual growth is a different matter. We must be purposeful about living our lives in a way that draws us closer to Christ and hastens our spiritual transformation. And we must certainly be disciplined in our own growth if we desire to help others grow as well.

Look again at Paul's word pictures in verses 3-7. How do these metaphors contribute to your understanding of discipleship?

Which of these metaphors best describes your understanding of the Christian life? Why?

Later in 2 Timothy 2, Paul again emphasized the need to be diligent as we follow Christ and help others do the same:

> Be diligent to present yourself to God as one approved, a worker who doesn't need to be ashamed, correctly teaching the word of truth.
> 2 TIMOTHY 2:15

What's interesting about this verse is that it comes in the middle of a negative example. Paul was correcting people in Timothy's congregation who had failed to be purposeful in their spiritual development, preferring instead to rely on "empty speech" (v. 16). This is one of the reasons why community is so important: we all get stalled in our spiritual growth at times, and we all need others to help us get back on track.

We must be purposeful about living our lives in a way that draws us closer to Christ and hastens our spiritual transformation.

Read 2 Timothy 2:14-19. How do these verses contribute to your understanding of discipleship?

How do you prefer to be corrected when you make mistakes?

ENGAGE

Use the space below to develop a spiritual family tree. Begin by recording the names of your spiritual grandparents, if you know them—those who were influential in leading to Christ the person or people who helped you become saved. Then record your spiritual parents. Also be sure to record others whom these people have helped encounter Christ; these would be your spiritual brothers and sisters.

Next, record your own name. Below that, record the names of people you are currently influencing as disciples of Jesus. Also add the names of people you hope will experience salvation in the future.

Why is it important for you to continue thinking about discipleship in terms of spiritual generations, rather than yourself as an individual?

PRAYER REQUESTS:

....

....

....

....

....

....

In addition to studying God's Word, work with your group leader to create a plan for personal study, worship, and application between now and the next session. Select from the following optional activities to match your personal preferences and available time.

⬆ Worship

☑ Read your Bible. Complete the reading plan on page 112.

☐ Spend time with God by engaging the devotional experience on page 113.

☐ Connect with God each day through prayer. Ask Him to provide opportunities for you to participate in His mission of making disciples.

➡⬅ Personal Study

☐ Read and interact with "Four Elements of Discipleship" on page 114.

☐ Read and interact with "Four Elements of Discipleship (Continued)" on page 116.

⬅➡ Application

☐ Write down your own definition for discipleship and place it somewhere you will see each day—the refrigerator, your car, your purse, your wallet, and so on.

☐ Make an appointment to talk with someone from your church's staff about discipleship in your congregation. Seek to get on the same page with your church leadership and see how you can contribute.

☐ Make a list of people who would be good candidates to disciple you (or to serve as a mentor). Pray through that list each day.

☐ Memorize 2 Timothy 2:2: "What you have heard from me in the presence of many witnesses, commit to faithful men who will be able to teach others also."

☐ Other:

 **WORSHIP**

READING PLAN

Read through the following Scripture passages this week. Use the space provided to record your thoughts and responses.

Day 1
John 13:1-20

Day 2
Proverbs 27:1-27

Day 3
Galatians 5:16-26

Day 4
Galatians 6:1-10

Day 5
John 15:1-17

Day 6
Acts 14:19-28

Day 7
2 Timothy 3:10-17

GROWTH ON THE VINE

As we've seen throughout this session, growth is a critical element of life as a disciple of Jesus. There's really no such thing as a stagnant follower of Christ—we are either growing closer to Him or fading further away.

Still, it's important to remember that our spiritual growth doesn't depend entirely on us. In fact, the opposite is true: our growth depends entirely on God's work in our lives through His Spirit inside us. Yes, we have a responsibility to obey God and carry out His work each day. But when it comes to our spiritual health and growth, we are like grapes resting on the vine:

> [5] "I am the vine; you are the branches. The one who remains in me and I in him produces much fruit, because you can do nothing without me. [6] If anyone does not remain in me, he is thrown aside like a branch and he withers. They gather them, throw them into the fire, and they are burned. [7] If you remain in me and my words remain in you, ask whatever you want and it will be done for you. [8] My Father is glorified by this: that you produce much fruit and prove to be my disciples.
>
> [9] "As the Father has loved me, I have also loved you. Remain in my love. [10] If you keep my commands you will remain in my love, just as I have kept my Father's commands and remain in his love.
>
> [11] "I have told you these things so that my joy may be in you and your joy may be complete.
>
> [12] "This is my command: Love one another as I have loved you. [13] No one has greater love than this: to lay down his life for his friends."
> JOHN 15:5-13

To what degree have you felt responsible for your own spiritual growth?

What steps can you take to let go of that responsibility and focus more fully on "remaining" in God's presence as the Vine?

FOUR ELEMENTS OF DISCIPLESHIP

Take a moment to review our earlier definition of discipleship: "the process of growing toward maturity as a follower of Jesus—and helping others do the same."

What would you add to or change about this definition?

How would you summarize your experiences with discipleship over the course of your life?

As you seek to obey Jesus by engaging the process of discipleship each day, remember these four important stages or elements of growing in Christ and helping others do the same.

1. Discipleship is progressive.

The Christian life has always been defined by forward momentum. We can't follow Jesus by standing still; we must go forward. In fact, this forward motion is a necessary ingredient in the idea of transformation—of changing from one thing into another. We can't change by standing still either.

Paul often emphasized the importance of spiritual transformation in the Christian's life, including here:

> We all, with unveiled faces, are looking as in a mirror at the glory of the Lord and are being transformed into the same image from glory to glory; this is from the Lord who is the Spirit.
> 2 CORINTHIANS 3:18

In what ways have you been transformed since following Christ?

In what ways do you hope to be transformed in the future?

Read Romans 12:1-2. What do these verses teach you about the process of spiritual transformation?

2. Discipleship requires discipline.

In many ways, living as a disciple of Jesus is a simple process. Our primary goal is to follow Christ each day and do the work He asks us to do. In doing so, we allow the Holy Spirit to continue His work in our hearts, transforming us so that we become more and more like Christ (see John 15:5-13).

On a more practical level, however, we need to remember that following Christ requires discipline on our part. That's because our natural inclination is to wander away from God and His work in our lives. We must be disciplined to stay on the right path and keep ourselves in a place where God's Spirit can work on our behalf.

That's why Paul so often wrote about discipline in his epistles to the early church:

> [7] But have nothing to do with pointless and silly myths. Rather, train yourself in godliness. [8] For the training of the body has limited benefit, but godliness is beneficial in every way, since it holds promise for the present life and also for the life to come. [9] This saying is trustworthy and deserves full acceptance. [10] For this reason we labor and strive, because we have put our hope in the living God, who is the Savior of all people, especially of those who believe.
> 1 TIMOTHY 4:7-10

What helps you stay disciplined in your walk with Christ?

What obstacles regularly chip away at your spiritual discipline?

FOUR ELEMENTS OF DISCIPLESHIP (CONTINUED)

3. Discipleship is relational.

Disciples of Jesus typically approach topics such as spiritual growth and transformation from the standpoint of individuals. Our society as a whole is individualistic, and so we naturally focus on what we ourselves need to do in order to stay on the right path as disciples of Jesus.

The Bible takes a different approach, however. The Scriptures mostly discuss spiritual growth and transformation in terms of the church as a community. In fact, that's how things were from the very start of the earliest church.

> *Read Acts 2:41-47. What do you find appealing about this description of the early church?*

> *How does your church congregation currently help you grow and mature as a disciple of Christ?*

Of course, we must never forget that our inclusion in the community of the church is a two-way street. Meaning, the church doesn't exist solely to help us in our journey with Christ. We're also responsible to support and equip other disciples as they seek to follow Him, as well—just as Philip did in the Book of Acts:

> 29 The Spirit told Philip, "Go and join that chariot." 30 When Philip ran up to it, he heard him reading the prophet Isaiah, and said, "Do you understand what you're reading?" 31 "How can I," he said, "unless someone guides me?" So he invited Philip to come up and sit with him.
> ACTS 8:29-31

> *When have you recently helped someone grow as a follower of Jesus or take a new step in their journey with Him?*

4. Discipleship includes replication.

We've seen that engaging a lifestyle of discipleship means helping others grow and mature as followers of Christ. But what does this "helping" look like on a daily basis? And, just as important, what is the long-term goal for our investments into the spiritual lives of others?

> *How would you answer those two questions?*

There is no "correct" way to equip and encourage others in their spiritual lives. Each disciple has different gifts and different weaknesses, which means each of us has a different way of helping others and being helped. However, one area of common ground for the process of discipleship is the investment of time in the lives of others.

Stated simply, we cannot help others grow spiritually at a distance. We need to connect with others in the body of Christ if we want to support their efforts to follow Christ.

> *Who are some people in your current spheres of influence in whom you'd like to invest your time and other resources?*

Things get easier when it comes to the second question mentioned above—identifying the long-term goal for our investments in the lives of others. That's because there *is* a correct answer to that question. Namely, our primary goal for investing in the spiritual lives of those we care about is to help them become disciples of Christ who can reproduce themselves.

That's the essence of what Paul wanted Timothy to understand in 2 Timothy 2:

> What you have heard from me in the presence of many witnesses, commit to faithful men who will be able to teach others also. (v. 2)

Remember that discipleship in the church is a matter of spiritual generations. Therefore, our goal in engaging the discipleship process is to become spiritual grandparents—to help raise disciples of Jesus who will also raise disciples of Jesus. This is the process that has spread the gospel to the ends of the earth throughout the history of the church.

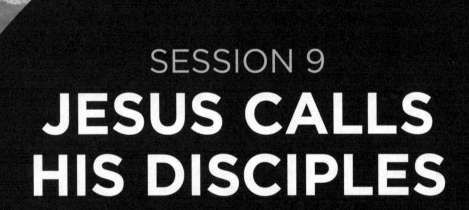

JESUS CALLS HIS DISCIPLES

Christ meets us where we are and
transforms us as we follow Him.

REFLECT

In the previous session we saw discipleship defined as *the process of growing toward maturity as a follower of Jesus and helping others do the same.* Yes, this process includes our personal growth towards Christ, but it can't be done apart from the body of Christ. Concepts like replication and modeling are very much a part of the discipleship equation.

As you prepare to explore how Jesus calls His disciples, take a moment to reflect on your experiences in recent days.

Which of the assignments did you explore this week? How did it go?

What did you learn or experience while reading the Bible?

What questions would you like to ask?

PRAY

Begin this session by connecting with God through prayer. Use the following guidelines as you speak with Him together:

- Praise God for giving you the opportunity to participate in His mission for the world.

- Express gratitude and thanks for the ways in which Jesus has called you as His disciple. Ask for clarity as you think through your earliest encounters with Him.

- Ask for wisdom to engage the Bible as you explore the theme of "calling" as a disciple of Christ.

INTRODUCTION

"I want YOU!"

You may be familiar with the famous U. S. Army recruitment poster of Uncle Sam—dressed in a blue suit, red tie, and white-starred hat—pointing directly at the viewer. His face is stern and serious. His posture is confident, and his white hair offers an air of both authority and experience. The full text reads, "I want YOU for the U. S. Army."

What you may not know is that the image for the poster was first created as a magazine cover for the July 6 issue of *Leslie's Weekly* in 1916 with the title, "What Are You Doing for Preparedness?" The image was adapted into the now-famous military poster and printed more than 4 million times between 1917 and 1918 as a recruitment tool during World War I. Because of its success, the poster was used again decades later when America entered World War II.

James Montgomery Flagg, the artist who originally created the image, later declared it to be "the most famous poster in the world."[1]

One reason the poster has maintained its popularity is because it reminds Americans of the deeper connection they have to their nation. They are not a loose collection of individuals running around and doing their own thing—though it may seem that way at times. They are Americans. In times of war or crisis, the poster is a call to action encouraging them not only to remember their national identity, but also to participate in defending the key ideas and principles that define their way of life.

When have you been excited to join a group or a cause?

When have you recently heard a recruitment slogan or call-to-action you found compelling?

As we'll see in this session, Jesus had different ways of recruiting His disciples during His public ministry on earth—but He did recruit them. He actively searched for followers and called them to join Him in His mission for the world.

Jesus still recruits His disciples today. In fact, the first step in living as a disciple of Christ is to answer His call.

KNOW THE STORY

In the early days of His public ministry, Jesus intentionally gathered a number of disciples around Him. As was the custom of rabbis in those days, Jesus intended for these young men to follow Him during His travels in order to both learn from Him and contribute to His ministry.

The following story shows how Jesus called two of those first disciples.

⁴³ The next day Jesus decided to leave for Galilee. He found Philip and told him, "Follow me." ⁴⁴ Now Philip was from Bethsaida, the hometown of Andrew and Peter. ⁴⁵ Philip found Nathanael and told him, "We have found the one Moses wrote about in the law (and so did the prophets): Jesus the son of Joseph, from Nazareth." ⁴⁶ "Can anything good come out of Nazareth?" Nathanael asked him. "Come and see," Philip answered.

⁴⁷ Then Jesus saw Nathanael coming toward him and said about him, "Here truly is an Israelite in whom there is no deceit." ⁴⁸ "How do you know me?" Nathanael asked. "Before Philip called you, when you were under the fig tree, I saw you," Jesus answered.

⁴⁹ "Rabbi," Nathanael replied, "You are the Son of God; you are the King of Israel!"

⁵⁰ Jesus responded to him, "Do you believe because I told you I saw you under the fig tree? You will see greater things than this." ⁵¹ Then he said, "Truly I tell you, you will see heaven opened and the angels of God ascending and descending on the Son of Man."
JOHN 1:43-51

What do these verses teach us about following Jesus?

How would you summarize the process through which Nathanael became a disciple?

UNPACK THE STORY

DISCIPLES HAVE AN ENCOUNTER WITH JESUS

The first step in becoming a disciple of Jesus is encountering Him in a deep and meaningful way. Nobody inherits a relationship with Jesus from their parents. Nobody earns their status as a disciple by attending church, doing good things, or avoiding bad things.

We become disciples of Christ when we experience Him in a way that changes our lives.

How has your life been changed by an encounter with Jesus?

Looking at John 1:43-51, it's interesting that Philip and Nathanael encountered Jesus in different ways. Philip received a direct call from Jesus. The Savior sought him out specifically and said: "Follow me." Nathanael, on the other hand, took a little more seasoning. He resisted Philip's attempts at evangelism, scoffing at the notion that the Messiah—the One prophesied in the Scriptures as the Savior of God's people—could come from an insignificant town like Nazareth. Even when he met Jesus, Nathanael challenged His assessment of his own character, asking, "How do you know me?"

> There's no template for receiving the call to follow Jesus. There are no magic words you *have* to say and no amount of steps you *must* follow in order to officially be considered a Christian.

Fortunately for Nathanael, he wasn't stubborn to the point of unbelief. When Jesus revealed Himself in a supernatural way, Nathanael responded by submitting himself before the Savior in worship and praise. "You are the Son of God!" he said, acknowledging that Jesus was indeed the Messiah. "You are the King of Israel!"

All of this tells us there's no template for receiving the call to follow Jesus. There are no magic words you *have* to say and no amount of steps you *must* follow in order to officially be considered a Christian. Instead, followers of Jesus are simply those who respond to His call.

What have you heard or been taught about the process of salvation?

What have you heard or been taught about what happens after salvation?

DISCIPLES ARE TRANSFORMED BY JESUS

We noted earlier that the first step in becoming a disciple of Jesus is encountering Him in a way that changes our lives. That was certainly the case with both Philip and Nathanael.

For example, notice that Philip responded to his encounter with Jesus by immediately seeking out the people he cared about and telling them about Jesus. He wanted them to have a similar encounter, and so he proclaimed the good news without shame or hesitation. He was transformed into an evangelist—seemingly in an instant.

Don't miss that. Too often Christians feel like they need to become "mature" before they can start sharing the gospel message. Too many disciples remain silent about their encounters with Jesus because they don't want to be seen as weird, or they don't want to impose on the time and beliefs of others.

The truth is that when we experience something that changes our lives for the better, we almost can't stop sharing the news. That's our natural reaction when we encounter something (or Someone) that brings us joy.

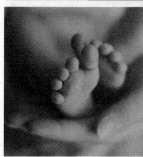

What emotions do you experience at the thought of sharing the gospel with those you care about?

Nathanael was also changed by his encounter with Jesus. When he was first told about Jesus, he was skeptical and a little sarcastic. But after meeting Jesus face-to-face, he responded with genuine worship. His behavior changed after responding to Jesus' call.

Of course, this was just the beginning of their spiritual transformation. Both Philip and Nathanael walked with Jesus for years before His death and resurrection. Afterward, they served faithfully in the early church and, according to church tradition, were eventually martyred for their faith in Christ. Throughout their lives, they continued to grow and mature as disciples of Jesus. The same should be true of us.

How have you experienced spiritual transformation?

> When we experience something that changes our lives for the better, we almost can't stop sharing the news. That's our natural reaction when we encounter something (or Someone) that brings us joy.

ENGAGE

Talking through your earliest encounters with Jesus is a great way to share the gospel message with those who need to hear it. You don't need a fancy testimony or a miniature sermon—simply share what you've experienced and how you've changed as a result.

Use the space below to outline or sketch your earliest encounters with Jesus and how those encounters have changed your life. After a few minutes, practice sharing your story with someone else.

Your First Encounters with Jesus

How You've Changed

PRAYER REQUESTS:

....

....

....

....

1. "The Most Famous Poster," American Treasures of the Library of Congress [online], 27 July 2010 [cited 2 September 2016]. Available from the Internet: *www.loc.gov*.

In addition to studying God's Word, work with your group leader to create a plan for personal study, worship, and application between now and the next session. Select from the following optional activities to match your personal preferences and available time.

⬆ Worship

☑ Read your Bible. Complete the reading plan on page 126.

☐ Spend time with God by engaging the devotional experience on page 127.

☐ Connect with God each day through prayer.

➡⬅ Personal Study

☐ Read and interact with "Disciples Have an Encounter with Jesus" on page 128.

☐ Read and interact with "Disciples Are Transformed by Jesus" on page 130.

⬅➡ Application

☐ Seek an opportunity to share your testimony this week. When you feel the time is right to share the gospel with someone in your life, talk openly about your experiences as a disciple of Jesus.

☐ Seek a fresh encounter with Jesus. It's easy to fall into a routine as a follower of Jesus. Therefore, make an effort to connect with Christ in a new or refreshing way.

☐ Memorize Mark 2:17: "When Jesus heard this, he told them, 'It is not those who are well who need a doctor, but those who are sick. I didn't come to call the righteous, but sinners.'"

☐ Journal about your earliest encounters with Jesus. Write down what you experienced when you first decided to follow Christ and how your life has changed since.

☐ Other:

 # WORSHIP

READING PLAN

Read through the following Scripture passages this week. Use the space provided to record your thoughts and responses.

Day 1
Matthew 5:1-16

Day 2
Luke 5:1-11

Day 3
Romans 5:1-21

Day 4
Romans 12:1-21

Day 5
Ephesians 4:17-32

Day 6
Colossians 3:1-17

Day 7
Revelation 21:1-27

JESUS' PRAYER

John 17 is an interesting chapter within the Gospels. The whole chapter is a long prayer recited by Jesus near the end of the Last Supper with His disciples. Jesus began by praying for Himself, asking that the Father would glorify Him even as He sought to glorify the Father by doing the work He had been called to do. Next, Jesus spent several verses praying for the disciples who were with Him.

Can you imagine what it would be like for Jesus to pray for you, specifically? Actually, that happened! After praying for the disciples physically present with Him at the time, Jesus prayed for all His disciples who would come later—including you.

Here's the first part of that prayer:

> [20] "I pray not only for these,
> but also for those who believe in me
> through their word.
> [21] May they all be one,
> as you, Father, are in me and I am in you.
> May they also be in us,
> so that the world may believe you sent me."
> JOHN 17:20-21

How does it make you feel to know that Jesus prayed for you before His sacrifice on the cross?

Read Jesus' entire prayer in John 17:20-26. What strikes you as most interesting in these verses? Why?

Spend a few moments echoing Jesus by praying through these verses, then listen for God to speak. What is He saying to your heart?

DISCIPLES HAVE AN ENCOUNTER WITH JESUS

Philip and Nathanael were personally called by Jesus to follow Him. The same was true of many others during Jesus' life, including men like Peter, James, John, and Matthew (see Matt. 10:2-4)—and also women such as Mary Magdalene, Joanna, and Susanna (see Luke 8:1-3). These individuals and many more served and supported Jesus during His ministry on earth.

What's interesting is that Jesus continued to call people to Himself even after His earthly ministry was over—even after His death, resurrection, and ascension had been accomplished. For example, Jesus personally and specifically reached out to a Pharisee named Saul of Tarsus:

> [1] Now Saul was still breathing threats and murder against the disciples of the Lord. He went to the high priest [2] and requested letters from him to the synagogues in Damascus, so that if he found any men or women who belonged to the Way, he might bring them as prisoners to Jerusalem. [3] As he traveled and was nearing Damascus, a light from heaven suddenly flashed around him. [4] Falling to the ground, he heard a voice saying to him, "Saul, Saul, why are you persecuting me?"
>
> [5] "Who are You, Lord?" Saul said.
>
> "I am Jesus, the one you are persecuting," he replied. [6] "But get up and go into the city, and you will be told what you must do."
> ACTS 9:1-6

Saul had been fully dedicated to his direction in life, which happened to involve "breathing threats and murder against the disciples of the Lord." When he encountered Jesus, however, and responded to Jesus' call, everything changed. Saul changed. He turned completely away from his old way of life and started down the path of following Christ. Today, we know Saul by his other name: the apostle Paul.

Paul's story is important because it reminds us of the need for repentance as we respond to Jesus' call.

What ideas or images come to mind when you hear the word "repent"?

To repent is to turn away from something or change your mind. And that's what Jesus calls us to do—He wants us to turn away from our old lives and old directions and to follow Him instead. In fact, according to the Gospel of Matthew, repentance was the primary theme of Jesus' early ministry:

> From then on Jesus began to preach, "Repent, because the kingdom of heaven has come near."
> MATTHEW 4:17

> [14] After John was arrested, Jesus went to Galilee, proclaiming the good news of God: [15] "The time is fulfilled, and the kingdom of God has come near. Repent and believe the good news!"
> MARK 1:14-15

What part did repentance play in your decision to follow Jesus?

Repentance is a necessary step in answering Jesus' call. However, it's not a step you only take once. We continue to wander away from God and from His mission for the world even after we choose to follow Him.

Therefore, to be a disciple of Jesus is to live a life of repentance in which we regularly turn away from our sin and choose once again to answer His call.

In what areas of life do you currently need to repent of your sin and return to Jesus?

What steps can you take to make sure repentance is a regular part of your spiritual life?

DISCIPLES ARE TRANSFORMED BY JESUS

It's true that the apostle Paul made a conscious decision to repent after encountering Jesus on the road to Damascus. He moved from completely opposing the cause of Christ—from persecuting and even murdering Jesus' disciples—to investing his resources in the advancement of that cause. He completely changed the trajectory of his life.

Yet it's also true that Paul didn't make such a drastic turn completely on his own. He was able to change the course of his life because *he* had been changed. Paul was transformed during his encounter with Jesus—he became someone different than he had been.

Today we refer to this phenomenon as spiritual transformation. Paul himself described it best during one of his letters to the early church:

> Therefore, if anyone is in Christ, he is a new creation; the old has passed away, and see, the new has come!
> 2 CORINTHIANS 5:17

What are some "old" things that have passed away in your life?

What "new" things have you experienced after encountering Jesus?

The type of transformation we experience immediately after encountering Jesus is known as justification. This is a legal term that highlights the guilt we all carry because of our sin. The good news of the gospel is that when we respond to God's call, we experience forgiveness from our sins in a way that changes our legal standing before God—we become justified in God's eyes because we are covered with the righteousness of Jesus. Paul explains:

> [9] How much more then, since we have now been declared righteous by his blood, will we be saved through him from wrath. [10] For if, while we were enemies, we were reconciled to God through the death of his Son, then how much more, having been reconciled, will we be saved by his life.
> ROMANS 5:9-10

Read the following Scripture passages and record how they contribute to your understanding of justification.

Hebrews 9:19-22

Romans 5:6-9

Galatians 2:15-16

While justification describes the spiritual transformation we experience immediately upon encountering Jesus and choosing to follow Him, that's not the end. In fact, to follow Jesus is to continually be transformed so that we become more and more like Him as we continue to follow Him. This ongoing transformation brings us closer and closer to the people God originally designed us to be.

This process is known as sanctification. Once again, Paul helps us understand:

> We all, with unveiled faces, are looking as in a mirror at the glory of the Lord and are being transformed into the same image from glory to glory; this is from the Lord who is the Spirit.
> 2 CORINTHIANS 3:18

Do you feel you've regularly experienced spiritual transformation as a follower of Jesus? Explain.

What obstacles are currently holding you back from having a deeper experience of spiritual transformation?

JESUS TEACHES HIS DISCIPLES

Disciples are called to learn about
Jesus and learn from Jesus.

REFLECT

In the previous session, we explored some of the different ways in which Jesus called His earliest disciples. We also continued to broaden our understanding of what it means to live as a disciple of Jesus by noting that all disciples have an encounter with Jesus that begins a process of spiritual transformation—a process that will continue to change us throughout our lives into the people we were originally created to be.

As you prepare to explore how Jesus teaches His disciples, take a moment to reflect on your experiences in recent days.

Which of the assignments did you explore this week? How did it go?

What did you learn or experience while reading the Bible?

What questions would you like to ask?

PRAY

Begin this session by connecting with God through prayer. Use the following guidelines as you speak with Him together:

- Thank God for the ways He has called you into His kingdom, and for His continued work of spiritual transformation in your life.

- Ask for God to speak clearly to your heart through His Word. Ask for wisdom to understand the truths you will encounter as you engage the Bible.

- Submit to God as your Teacher and commit to applying what you learn throughout this study.

INTRODUCTION

When you hear the word *counterfeit*, what's the first thing that pops into your head? It's money, right? Criminals produce counterfeit money and try to pass it off as genuine bills, seeking to trick merchants into accepting the fake currency.

Because counterfeit money is a real threat, cashiers and other people who deal regularly with cash need to learn how to discern authentic currency from counterfeit. Bank tellers, specifically, are trained to detect counterfeit bills so that their bank isn't left in the lurch with fraudulent money.

The way bank tellers are trained to spot counterfeits is interesting. They don't learn about methods for counterfeiting money. They don't get profiles on the people who produce counterfeit currency. They don't even spend time studying fake $100 bills. Instead, bank employees learn to spot counterfeit currency *by intensely studying the real thing*. They train their eyes and their senses by watching, smelling, feeling, and continually interacting with real money in order to spot fake money whenever it comes along.

The same is true for discipleship. If we want to know what a disciple should look like—what they should believe and do—we need to know the One we're called to follow.

The scary thing about counterfeits is that they look nearly identical to the real thing. On the surface, there appears to be no difference. Why is that scary? Because we could easily find ourselves going through the motions as disciples of Jesus, yet be false at the core. Many of the activities of a disciple can be practiced without integrity, and yet still appear to the world as authentic.

What are some common actions of Jesus' disciples that are easy to counterfeit?

Why is hypocrisy dangerous in God's kingdom?

It's time to study the real thing. In this session, we'll focus on Jesus as our Teacher. We'll seek to learn from Him—and learn about Him—as we explore our responsibilities in the process of moving forward as disciples of Christ.

KNOW THE STORY

Jesus' words in Matthew 5–7 are known today as the Sermon on the Mount. This is no doubt the most famous sermon ever preached, and it was delivered by the greatest Teacher who ever lived; therefore, it's worthy of our attention. But as we explore Jesus' sermon, let's focus on two key passages that are often overlooked.

[1] When he saw the crowds, he went up on the mountain, and after he sat down, his disciples came to him. [2] Then he began to teach them.
MATTHEW 5:1-2

[24] "Therefore, everyone who hears these words of mine and acts on them will be like a wise man who built his house on the rock. [25] The rain fell, the rivers rose, and the winds blew and pounded that house. Yet it didn't collapse, because its foundation was on the rock. [26] But everyone who hears these words of mine and doesn't act on them will be like a foolish man who built his house on the sand. [27] The rain fell, the rivers rose, the winds blew and pounded that house, and it collapsed. It collapsed with a great crash." [28] When Jesus had finished saying these things, the crowds were astonished at his teaching, [29] because he was teaching them like one who had authority, and not like their scribes.
MATTHEW 7:24-29

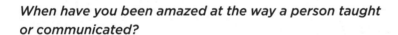

When have you been amazed at the way a person taught or communicated?

How would you summarize the primary message of these Scripture passages?

Both of these passages help us grasp the necessity of learning from Jesus—and of taking action to obey what we learn—as we follow Him.

UNPACK THE STORY

DISCIPLES ADOPT A POSTURE TO LEARN

One of the hallmarks of Jesus' sermon was how He regularly turned common wisdom on its head in order to show us what a true disciple looks like. Jesus kept repeating the phrase, "You have heard that it was said," before referencing interpretations of the Old Testament law or cultural norms. Then He would ratchet up the tension by saying, "But I tell you."

Again and again, Jesus called His disciples to a higher level of obedience. He pushed them to shape the culture around them rather than just follow what everyone else was doing.

Read Matthew 5:1-12. Which of Jesus' statements do you find most countercultural? Why?

As wonderful as it is to read Jesus' teaching, don't miss those first two verses:

> ¹ When he saw the crowds, he went up on the mountain, and after he sat down, his disciples came to him. ² Then he began to teach them.
> MATTHEW 5:1-2

Notice that not everyone heard Jesus' teaching. Not everyone followed Him up the mountain. But His disciples did. They had already abandoned much of their "normal" lives in order to travel with Jesus. And now they trekked up the side of a mountain to sit at His feet. Jesus' disciples placed themselves in a posture to learn. Therefore, they were blessed by His teaching.

Jesus' disciples placed themselves in a posture to learn. Therefore, they were blessed by His teaching.

In what settings or situations do you most often hear from Jesus in a meaningful way?

How can you intentionally place yourself in a posture to learn from Jesus this week?

Adopting a posture to learn from Jesus is a necessary step for His disciples. But it's not the final step in the process.

DISCIPLES OBEY WHAT THEY LEARN

When you think about it, there's a big difference between students and disciples. Both groups are interested in learning from a teacher. However, students learn for the sake of information; they learn in order to pass a test or achieve a degree. Disciples, on the other hand, learn for the sake of obedience. They learn in order to take action.

That's why Jesus regularly warned people to be conscious of their fruit. For example, look at what He said in Matthew 7:

> ¹⁵ "Be on your guard against false prophets who come to you in sheep's clothing but inwardly are ravaging wolves. ¹⁶ You'll recognize them by their fruit. Are grapes gathered from thornbushes or figs from thistles? ¹⁷ In the same way, every good tree produces good fruit, but a bad tree produces bad fruit."
> MATTHEW 7:15-17

When have you experienced the tension between believing something to be true and acting on that belief?

The storms of life are often unkind to followers of Jesus. Therefore, we need a firm foundation—we need something solid on which we can build our lives, weather the storms, and continue to participate in Jesus' mission for the world. Clearly, the teachings of Jesus offer the only sure foundation on which we can build. He is the Rock.

At the same time, Jesus' teachings only serve as a usable foundation *when they are acted upon*. Obedience is necessary if we want to avoid building on sand.

The teachings of Jesus offer the only sure foundation on which we can build. He is the Rock.

What are some key teachings of Jesus that all disciples should believe? (Skim through Matt. 5–7 for examples.)

What actions are required or implied by these teachings?

ENGAGE

Being part of a community is a great way to engage Jesus' teaching in a way that fosters both understanding and obedience. Joining with others to study God's Word is helpful when passages are especially deep or difficult to understand. And being in community offers a number of opportunities for accountability—it makes it more difficult for us to actively ignore what we know to be true.

For these reasons and more, work together to engage the following portion of Jesus' teaching:

> 25 "Therefore I tell you: Don't worry about your life, what you will eat or what you will drink; or about your body, what you will wear. Isn't life more than food and the body more than clothing? 26 Consider the birds of the sky: They don't sow or reap or gather into barns, yet your heavenly Father feeds them. Aren't you worth more than they? 27 Can any of you add one moment to his life-span by worrying? 28 And why do you worry about clothes? Observe how the wildflowers of the field grow: They don't labor or spin thread. 29 Yet I tell you that not even Solomon in all his splendor was adorned like one of these. 30 If that's how God clothes the grass of the field, which is here today and thrown into the furnace tomorrow, won't he do much more for you—you of little faith? 31 So don't worry, saying, 'What will we eat?' or 'What will we drink?' or 'What will we wear?' 32 For the Gentiles eagerly seek all these things, and your heavenly Father knows that you need them. 33 But seek first the kingdom of God and his righteousness, and all these things will be provided for you. 34 Therefore don't worry about tomorrow, because tomorrow will worry about itself. Each day has enough trouble of its own."
> MATTHEW 6:25-34

What are the key truths contained in this passage?
How can you apply these truths in your life this week?

PRAYER REQUESTS:

....

....

....

In addition to studying God's Word, work with your group leader to create a plan for personal study, worship, and application between now and the next session. Select from the following optional activities to match your personal preferences and available time.

⬆ Worship

☑ Read your Bible. Complete the reading plan on page 140.

☐ Spend time with God by engaging the devotional experience on page 141.

☐ Connect with God each day through prayer. Specifically, concentrate on smaller prayers throughout the day, asking that Jesus would help you remain in a posture to hear from Him and obey His teaching.

➡ ⬅ Personal Study

☐ Read and interact with "Disciples Adopt a Posture to Learn" on page 142.

☐ Read and interact with "Disciples Obey What They Learn" on page 144.

⬅ ➡ Application

☐ Read through the entire Sermon on the Mount (Matt. 5–7) this week. Consider reading it out loud as a way to increase your concentration on the text.

☐ Invite a friend or family member to study God's Word with you. Approaching the Bible in community can help you maintain a posture that's ready to learn.

☐ Memorize Matthew 7:24: "Therefore, everyone who hears these words of mine and acts on them will be like a wise man who built his house on the rock."

☐ To continue your journal, write down the different ways you see the fruit of the Spirit manifested in yourself and in the people around you (see Gal. 5:22-23). Be intentional to seek out examples and jot them down.

☐ Other:

 # WORSHIP

READING PLAN

Read through the following Scripture passages this week. Use the space provided to record your thoughts and responses.

Day 1
Psalm 119:1-24

Day 2
Psalm 119:25-48

Day 3
Psalm 119:49-80

Day 4
Psalm 119:81-104

Day 5
Psalm 119:105-136

Day 6
Psalm 119:137-160

Day 7
Psalm 119:161-176

YOUR TRUE HEART

We've seen how important it is for our actions to match our beliefs—or what we claim to be our beliefs. The difficulty in achieving this is that we often deceive ourselves. We shy away from the truth about what we believe and what we do.

The prophet Jeremiah told us why:

> The heart is more deceitful than anything else,
> and incurable—who can understand it?
> JEREMIAH 17:9

How easily we let ourselves off the hook. We're quick to grant ourselves grace and mercy because we believe that deep down we really are good people with good intentions. We believe the best about ourselves and hope that everything will come out alright in the end. This is dangerous.

Fortunately, Jeremiah also offered the solution to our problem:

> I, the LORD, examine the mind,
> I test the heart
> to give to each according to his way,
> according to what his actions deserve.
> JEREMIAH 17:10

Take a moment right now to pause and seek God's presence. Ask Him to "test" your true heart—to help you see more clearly how your actions match up with what you say you believe.

What has God revealed to you?

What do you need to do in response to that revelation?

DISCIPLES ADOPT A POSTURE TO LEARN

If you've ever had a conversation with someone who was constantly checking his or her phone, then you know how frustrating it can be to have half of a person's attention. Because, honestly, having half of someone's attention feels like having none of it. It's offensive, distracting, and unhelpful when a person is "there but not there." In the end, it costs everyone unnecessary extra time and attention to move forward.

Do you think God ever feels that way about us? Is it possible He says, "I'm willing to teach, but you are":

- Consumed by your job.
- Distracted by stress.
- Pursuing pleasure.
- Ignoring My Word.

The posture of our lives will tell God whether we really want to hear what He has to say. True disciples position themselves to hear from God. They structure their lives so that when God speaks, they're ready to listen and respond.

> *What habits or activities—even "good" ones—prevent you from positioning yourself to hear from God?*

Disciples of Jesus know it's not enough to simply "want" His truth. They go after it. They sacrifice for it. That's because receiving truth isn't a passive experience. To learn from Jesus is to actively bend your life around what matters most. In short, we don't grow as disciples by listening to a sermon every week or even attending a Bible study.

Rather, disciples learn and grow by making small choices each day—sometimes each hour—to actively trust Jesus and listen for His voice.

> *How satisfied are you with your current efforts to learn from Jesus?*

1	2	3	4	5	6	7	8	9	10
Not satisfied									Very satisfied

In Matthew 5, we saw Jesus' disciples trek up a mountain in order to hear His teaching in what we now call the Sermon on the Mount. That wasn't the only time Jesus' disciples had to make an effort to experience Him more deeply:

> ¹ After six days Jesus took Peter, James, and his brother John and led them up on a high mountain by themselves. ² He was transfigured in front of them, and his face shone like the sun; his clothes became as white as the light.
> MATTHEW 17:1-2

Once again, the disciples put real effort into following Jesus. They sacrificed their time and energy in order to be in the right place to learn from Him—and the reward was incredible.

Read the entire experience in Matthew 17:1-13. What did the disciples learn from Jesus in these verses?

When have you experienced Jesus as your Teacher?

It's not easy to follow Jesus. You'll sometimes need to scale a mountain just to hear from Him. But the effort will be more than worth it.

Unfortunately, some disciples stop at base camp at the bottom of that mountain and find great comfort in never exercising their faith, never growing, and never hearing from God. Others begin the ascent, but the demands of life (or their own bad habits) drag them down well before the summit. But the ones who complete the journey up the mountain will hear from God. And His voice will give them peace, comfort, and joy.

How will you remind yourself to make daily (or hourly) decisions to actively trust Jesus and listen for His voice?

DISCIPLES OBEY WHAT THEY LEARN

There are many scary verses in the Bible. But this verse near the end of Jesus' Sermon on the Mount may be one of the scariest:

> Not everyone who says to me, "Lord, Lord," will enter the kingdom of
> heaven, but only the one who does the will of my Father in heaven.
> MATTHEW 7:21

Maybe you're wondering, *What did Jesus mean when He said to do "the will of my Father in heaven"?* The answer is that obeying God goes beyond doing the right things. In fact, God has always been unimpressed with people who do the right things for the wrong reasons:

> [11] "What are all your sacrifices to me?"
> asks the LORD.
> "I have had enough of burnt offerings and rams
> and the fat of well-fed cattle;
> I have no desire for the blood of bulls,
> lambs, or male goats...."

> [15] "When you spread out your hands in prayer,
> I will refuse to look at you;
> even if you offer countless prayers,
> I will not listen.
> Your hands are covered with blood."
> ISAIAH 1:11,15

What emotions do you experience when you read these verses from Matthew 7 and Isaiah 1? Why?

Rewrite Isaiah 1:11 based on your own experiences with church today.

During the Sermon on the Mount, Jesus proclaimed that our fruit is what separates true disciples from those who are simply going through the motions. Interestingly, Jesus wasn't teaching something entirely new. He was expanding on a similar idea from Isaiah 1.

> **Read Isaiah 1:16-20. What kinds of "fruit" from following God are mentioned in these verses?**

Jesus' disciples also emphasized the theme of spiritual fruit when they wrote later portions of the New Testament. The most famous example came from the apostle Paul:

> [22] But the fruit of the Spirit is love, joy, peace, patience, kindness, goodness, faithfulness, [23] gentleness, and self-control. The law is not against such things.
> GALATIANS 5:22-23

Remember that obeying God involves more than snap decisions or brief spurts of righteousness. We don't produce fruit simply by saying, "I'm going to be kind or peaceful for a few minutes so that I can prove I love God." Instead, the fruit of the Spirit will be naturally and automatically cultivated in our lives when we genuinely follow Jesus, submit to His teaching, and grow to be more and more like Him.

In other words, we don't follow Jesus by trying to do more good things. Rather, the fruit of the Spirit provides evidence that God is working to transform our hearts.

> **Which elements of the fruit of the Spirit are most evident in your life?**

> **Which elements of the fruit of the Spirit are least evident in your life?**

JESUS EQUIPS HIS DISCIPLES

Jesus gives us what we need to engage

His mission for the world.

REFLECT

We saw previously that disciples of Jesus need to intentionally adopt a posture in which they can learn from Him. In addition, we saw that the process of learning is only complete—and only results in true transformation—when it's connected to obedience in our actions. The more we learn from Jesus and obey His teaching, the more fruit we'll produce for His kingdom.

As you prepare to explore how Jesus equips His disciples, take a moment to reflect on your experiences in recent days.

Which of the assignments did you explore this week? How did it go?

What did you learn or experience while reading the Bible?

What questions would you like to ask?

PRAY

Begin this session by connecting with God through prayer. Use the following guidelines as you speak with Him together:

- Thank God for what you've learned and experienced in recent weeks.

- Express your desire to be equipped as a participant in Jesus' mission for the world. Be honest about what you'd like to gain and where you'd like to grow in order to participate more fully.

- Ask for courage to not only understand what you encounter in God's Word this session, but also to obey what you learn.

INTRODUCTION

Do you DIY?

DIY is an acronym that stands for "Do it yourself." It refers to the phenomenon of people tackling home-improvement projects themselves whenever possible, rather than calling plumbers, carpenters, and other professionals. DIY people take pride in successfully completing a project and saving money at the same time.

Of course, millions of people probably attempt to tackle home-improvement projects every week. But just attempting a project doesn't make you DIY. In fact, one main difference exists between DIY people and non-DIY people—tools.

You can usually tell if a person is really into the DIY experience by the tools he or she uses. DIY people have learned from experience that the right tool is often the difference between a job well done and an expensive mess. For that reason, DIY people equip themselves with the tools they need to accomplish their goals.

When have you recently felt equipped to accomplish an important task?

Here's a question you should consider honestly: Would Jesus give you a job to do without also equipping you to be successful? Thankfully, the answer is no.

In this session, we'll see how Jesus equipped His disciples even as He sent them out to fulfill a specific mission. This was an important moment for the early disciples, and it carries a lot of implications for us as we seek to participate in Jesus' mission for the world.

In what ways would you like to feel more equipped as you participate in Jesus' mission for the world?

KNOW THE STORY

Matthew 10 marks a turning point in the lives of Jesus' earliest disciples. Until that moment, the disciples had spent most of their time with Jesus. They traveled with Him, served with Him, ate with Him, and even celebrated with Him. In Matthew 10, however, Jesus sent them out in pairs to minister away from Him.

> [1] Summoning his twelve disciples, he gave them authority over unclean spirits, to drive them out and to heal every disease and sickness....
>
> [5] Jesus sent out these twelve after giving them instructions: "Don't take the road that leads to the Gentiles, and don't enter any Samaritan town. [6] Instead, go to the lost sheep of the house of Israel. [7] As you go, proclaim: 'The kingdom of heaven has come near.' [8] Heal the sick, raise the dead, cleanse those with leprosy, drive out demons. Freely you received, freely give. [9] Don't acquire gold, silver, or copper for your money-belts. [10] Don't take a traveling bag for the road, or an extra shirt, sandals, or a staff, for the worker is worthy of his food. [11] When you enter any town or village, find out who is worthy, and stay there until you leave. [12] Greet a household when you enter it, [13] and if the household is worthy, let your peace be on it; but if it is unworthy, let your peace return to you. [14] If anyone does not welcome you or listen to your words, shake the dust off your feet when you leave that house or town. [15] Truly I tell you, it will be more tolerable on the day of judgment for the land of Sodom and Gomorrah than for that town."
> MATTHEW 10:1,5-15

What emotions would you have experienced if you received these instructions from Jesus?

Which part of these instructions seems most difficult? Why?

UNPACK THE STORY

JESUS PROVIDES WHAT WE NEED

In our efforts to live as His disciples, Jesus equips us with a number of important resources. We have the Bible, for example, which serves as our foundation for understanding God, the world, and history. We also have access to the church—to a community of brothers and sisters working together in service to God. And we have our own unique mix of talents and abilities.

How have your talents and abilities empowered you to participate in Jesus' mission for the world?

Still, how would you like to receive the following instructions from Jesus?

> Heal the sick, raise the dead, cleanse those with leprosy, drive out demons. Freely you received, freely give.
> MATTHEW 10:8

We must never lose sight of the crucial truth that our most important resource in following Jesus is our access to Jesus Himself.

If you don't think you could handle these commands—you're absolutely right. People don't possess such supernatural abilities on their own. The only way Jesus' disciples were able to perform these miraculous feats was because Jesus Himself had granted them His power and authority: "Summoning his twelve disciples, he gave them authority over unclean spirits, to drive them out and to heal every disease and sickness" (Matt. 10:1).

Disciples today are also called to achieve an incredible goal—the advancement of God's kingdom throughout the world. For that reason, we must never lose sight of the crucial truth that our most important resource in following Jesus is our access to Jesus Himself.

When have you felt empowered to take action or make the right choice because of your relationship with Jesus?

Jesus equipped the disciples with His power and presence in order for them to obey His commands. The great news is that He does the same for us.

JESUS CLARIFIES WHAT WE DON'T NEED

Not only did Jesus equip the disciples with His power and presence, He also made sure they understood what they *did not* need in order to carry out His mission:

> ⁹ Don't acquire gold, silver, or copper for your money-belts.
> ¹⁰ Don't take a traveling bag for the road, or an extra shirt, sandals, or a staff, for the worker is worthy of his food.
> MATTHEW 10:9-10

Does that mean you should get rid of your suitcase the next time you go on a mission trip? Or that you should abandon your debit card when you serve in your church? Not exactly.

Jesus was calling the disciples to let go of what made them feel safe and comfortable before they went on mission. Why? Because He wanted them to rely completely on His power and presence. He wanted them to set aside their own resources so they would be free to demonstrate faith in His provision.

When was the last time you took a leap of faith? What happened next?

As modern Christians, we need to understand that what Jesus is calling us to do is far beyond our own abilities and resources. To be frank, if your concept of following Jesus fits neatly into our culture's conception of a "normal" life, you need to stretch your understanding of what it means to be a disciple of Christ.

Following Jesus should force us to rely completely on Him.

Following Jesus should force us to rely completely on Him.

What are your current goals as a disciple of Jesus?

In what ways have you been dependent on Jesus in order to achieve those goals?

ENGAGE

Setting goals is a good practice for most areas of life. If something is worth an investment of your time, it makes sense to plan out what you want to achieve or how you want to grow. For these reasons, it can be beneficial to set goals concerning your walk and growth as a disciple of Jesus. But your goals for following Christ should be vastly different than your goals for your budget or for learning a new language. Why? Because your goals as a Christian should be big, bold, and audacious. In fact, the goals you set as a follower of Jesus should be impossible to achieve without the intervention and support of Jesus.

That being the case, take a few moments to practice setting goals as a Christian. Work with your group to create short-term and long-term dreams that will connect with your passions and will force you to rely on Christ.

How would you like to grow as a follower of Christ?

Short-term goals	Long-term goals

What would you like to achieve as a follower of Christ?

Short-term goals	Long-term goals

PRAYER REQUESTS:

WEEKLY ACTIVITIES

In addition to studying God's Word, work with your group leader to create a plan for personal study, worship, and application between now and the next session. Select from the following optional activities to match your personal preferences and available time.

⬆ Worship

☑ Read your Bible. Complete the reading plan on page 154.

☐ Connect with God each day through prayer. As you make a conscious effort to rely on God throughout the day, it's important that you stay connected with Him through regular times of prayer.

☐ Spend time with God by engaging the devotional experience on page 155.

➡ ⬅ Personal Study

☐ Read and interact with "Jesus Provides What We Need" on page 156.

☐ Read and interact with "Jesus Clarifies What We Don't Need" on page 158.

⬅ ➡ Application

☐ Take a prayer walk through your neighborhood or workplace. As you walk in a specific area, share with God your hopes and dreams for ministering in that area.

☐ Work with your family to evaluate whether any "extras" are holding you back from fully relying on Jesus as you follow Him. Be open to difficult decisions.

☐ Memorize Matthew 10:27-28: "What I tell you in the dark, speak in the light. What you hear in a whisper, proclaim on the housetops. Don't fear those who kill the body but are not able to kill the soul; rather, fear him who is able to destroy both soul and body in hell."

☐ Update your journal by writing down your prayer requests each day (or each week) and then recording the answers to those requests each time God responds. This is a great way to see clearly how well God provides for you.

☐ Other:

 **WORSHIP**

READING PLAN

Read through the following Scripture passages this week. Use the space provided to record your thoughts and responses.

Day 1
Genesis 22:1-18

Day 2
Genesis 50:1-21

Day 3
Exodus 6:28–7:13

Day 4
Joshua 2:1-24

Day 5
1 Samuel 17:1-37

Day 6
John 4:1-26

Day 7
Philippians 2:1-18

MORE THAN YOU NEED

In your attempts to live as a follower of Jesus, you may have felt inadequate or unprepared in certain situations. You may even have felt ineffective or unworthy as a disciple. Perhaps you feel that way now.

Whether or not you struggle with those emotions, the truth is that you are indeed inadequate to follow Jesus in your own strength. You are unprepared based on your own knowledge. Similarly, you will be ineffective when you attempt to take matters into your own hands. And you are certainly unworthy to live as a disciple of Christ, who is your Master as well as the all-knowing, ever-present, all-powerful God.

It's not just you, though. All Christians are woefully unable to follow Jesus in and of themselves. That's the bad news.

The good news is that Jesus has called you to follow Him in spite of your limitations. And because of His presence in your life, you are neither inadequate nor unprepared. Because He is the source of your strength, you are neither ineffective nor unworthy. You can live successfully and powerfully as disciples of Jesus because you are connected to Him.

He's all you need!

In what ways do you feel weak or inadequate as a follower of Jesus?

In what situations, settings, or circumstances do you often struggle to live boldly and confidently as a disciple of Christ?

How will you spend time in Jesus' presence this week in order to draw strength and confidence from Him?

JESUS PROVIDES WHAT WE NEED

When we allow Jesus to be the primary Source and Supplier for fulfilling our mission, He equips us in a number of important ways. For example, Paul wrote the following description of the "armor of God," which we receive as we are "strengthened by the Lord":

> ¹⁰ Finally, be strengthened by the Lord and by his vast strength. ¹¹ Put on the full armor of God so that you can stand against the schemes of the devil. ¹² For our struggle is not against flesh and blood, but against the rulers, against the authorities, against the cosmic powers of this darkness, against evil, spiritual forces in the heavens. ¹³ For this reason take up the full armor of God, so that you may be able to resist in the evil day, and having prepared everything, to take your stand. ¹⁴ Stand, therefore, with truth like a belt around your waist, righteousness like armor on your chest, ¹⁵ and your feet sandaled with readiness for the gospel of peace. ¹⁶ In every situation take up the shield of faith with which you can extinguish all the flaming arrows of the evil one. ¹⁷ Take the helmet of salvation and the sword of the Spirit—which is the word of God.
> EPHESIANS 6:10-17

What do you think Paul meant by "our struggle" in verse 12?

How have you benefited from the armor described in verses 14-17?

With which pieces of armor would you like to be equipped in a more powerful way?

Remember that Jesus equips us with His armor through "his vast strength." You can't will yourself into having more faith or more righteousness. Rather, just like the fruit of the Spirit, you'll be equipped with the armor of God as you intentionally connect with other Christians, study God's Word, pray, and obey Him.

We saw in Matthew 10 how Jesus sent the disciples out in pairs to minister in their communities. After the disciples returned, Jesus sought to equip them further by deepening their relationship with Him:

> 30 The apostles gathered around Jesus and reported to him all that they had done and taught. 31 He said to them, "Come away by yourselves to a remote place and rest for a while." For many people were coming and going, and they did not even have time to eat.
> MARK 6:30-31

Don't miss this important truth: Jesus equips us with everything we need to participate in His mission for the world, but this equipping happens primarily as we spend time in His presence. That was true of Jesus' earliest disciples, and it's true of His disciples today.

How have you recently made time to connect with Jesus in a deep and personal way?

When will you make time this week to connect with Jesus?

Remember that we don't have to engage God's mission on our own authority. In fact, *we can't* engage God's mission on our own authority. But the great news is that we've been given the authority of Jesus in order to participate in His mission (see Matt. 10:1). We're weak, but He's strong. We're fragile, but He's powerful. We fumble over our words, but He speaks for us (see Matt. 10:20). We have unconvincing arguments, but He changes hard hearts (see Ezek. 36:26).

Your mission is not your own, and your authority is not your own. All you're called to do is humbly obey.

How is God calling you to obey Him right now? (Consider spending time in prayer as you contemplate this question.)

PERSONAL STUDY

JESUS CLARIFIES WHAT WE DON'T NEED

One of the challenges that has hampered followers of Jesus throughout history is that it's so often easier to ask questions about God's commands than to obey them. It's easier to complain than to be generous. It's easier to stand in judgment than to talk of grace or offer hope.

In other words, our hearts are great at finding excuses for why we can't participate in Jesus' mission:

- I'll lose my job.
- I don't know enough Scripture.
- I don't have the right gifts.
- I'll do it tomorrow.

What excuses do you use when you don't want to obey what God is asking of you?

Jesus' original disciples looked for the same excuses we do. That's why Jesus told them not to take any "extras" as they set out to make an impact in their communities (see Matt. 10:9-10). No money to buy shortcuts. No staff for protection from enemies. No extra clothes to stay comfortable if something wore out. Instead of relying on their "extras" to carry them through their journeys, Jesus commanded the disciples to rely on Him.

Which "extras" eat up a large percentage of your time and attention throughout the week?

What do you typically rely on—money, connections, family, and so on— to carry you through difficult situations?

Two stories from the Gospel of Luke highlight some additional baggage we don't need to carry when we follow Jesus. First, we don't need to retain our sense of self-importance:

> ⁴⁶ An argument started among them about who was the greatest of them. ⁴⁷ But Jesus, knowing their inner thoughts, took a little child and had him stand next to him. ⁴⁸ He told them, "Whoever welcomes this little child in my name welcomes me. And whoever welcomes me welcomes him who sent me. For whoever is least among you—this one is great."
> LUKE 9:46-48

As a follower of Jesus, you will be tempted to compare yourself to other disciples. Such comparisons are rarely helpful, and they often cause great damage.

How often do you compare yourself to other Christians?

1	2	3	4	5	6	7	8	9	10
Rarely									Often

The second type of baggage we don't need to carry as followers of Jesus is our self-righteous behavior and tendency to judge those with whom we disagree:

> ⁴⁹ John responded, "Master, we saw someone driving out demons in your name, and we tried to stop him because he does not follow us."
>
> ⁵⁰ "Don't stop him," Jesus told him, "because whoever is not against you is for you."
> LUKE 9:49-50

How often do you stand in judgment over the way others follow Christ?

1	2	3	4	5	6	7	8	9	10
Rarely									Often

It's easy to fall into the trap of believing that our community is the only community that follows Jesus correctly—that we're the only ones who worship rightly, behave properly, believe the right doctrines, and witness the best way. The truth is, we're all servants in submission to our Master and Lord.

JESUS SENDS HIS DISCIPLES

Christ calls us to take the gospel to the world.

REFLECT

The goal from the previous session was to see the great news that Jesus gives us everything we need to engage His mission in the world. We don't have to rely on our own power to accomplish this enormous task. Before you dive deeper into the ways Jesus actively sends us into the world, take a moment to reflect on your experiences in recent days.

Which of the assignments did you explore this week? How did it go?

What did you learn or experience while reading the Bible?

What questions would you like to ask?

PRAY

Begin this session by connecting with God through prayer. Use the following guidelines as you speak with Him together:

- Thank God for what He has taught you during this study and for the ways He has helped you grow in your knowledge of Him.

- Pray that God would bless you with the courage necessary to act on what you've learned in recent sessions, and especially on what you will learn in this final session.

- Commit now to making the most of your time as you conclude this study on what it means to live and grow as a disciple of Christ.

INTRODUCTION

As a stunt man for Universal Studios, Michael Brady specialized in skydiving. During a filming session in Benson, Arizona, Michael was preparing to parachute onto the top of a moving train when he slipped and fell from a high elevation. He struck his head on landing and died instantly.

That wasn't the end of his story, however. Michael's body was taken to the University Medical Center in Tucson, where his heart was removed and transplanted into the body of another man, Bill Wohl, who had suffered heart failure more than five months earlier.

Six months and one day after receiving his new heart, Bill Wohl opened a letter from Michael Brady's family, which included a picture of Michael and some background information. Bill was shocked to learn he'd been given the heart of a 36-year-old Hollywood stuntman. "I looked at this picture," Bill said, "at this incredibly good-looking, super-fit, super-athletic guy. And I thought: *Are you kidding me? That's whose heart I've got?*"

Before his heart transplant, Bill Wohl had been a Type A, overweight, money-obsessed businessman pursuing a jet-setter lifestyle. Today he works part time, spending most of his new-found energy winning speed and performance medals in swimming, cycling, and track.

When interviewed by a reporter in his Scottsdale condo, Bill Wohl spoke passionately about the blessing he'd received: "Every day, all day, I thank God for Michael Brady." Glancing at his many medals won through athletic competitions, Wohl added, "When I ride, when I work out—the biggest thing is to honor him."[1]

In other words, Bill Wohl was dramatically changed by a new heart.

***What are the biggest changes you've experienced in your
time as a follower of Jesus?***

Like Bill Wohl, you have received a new heart as a disciple of Jesus. You are in the process of being transformed from the inside out. When Christ's heart beats in your chest, you will live to honor Him each day and you will share His passion to take the gospel to the world.

KNOW THE STORY

Jesus' earliest disciples experienced a roller-coaster ride during the final weeks of His public ministry. First, Jesus' death on the cross sent them into confusion and deep despair. Second, His resurrection lifted them back into the clouds of joy. Finally, His ascension ushered in the sobering reality that the disciples would continue carrying out Jesus' mission without His physical presence and leadership.

Before Jesus returned to heaven, however, He gathered His remaining followers in order to summarize the mission for His disciples and deliver final instructions. Today we refer to Jesus' final words as the Great Commission.

> ¹⁶ The eleven disciples traveled to Galilee, to the mountain where Jesus had directed them. ¹⁷ When they saw him, they worshiped, but some doubted. ¹⁸ Jesus came near and said to them, "All authority has been given to me in heaven and on earth. ¹⁹ Go, therefore, and make disciples of all nations, baptizing them in the name of the Father and of the Son and of the Holy Spirit, ²⁰ teaching them to observe everything I have commanded you. And remember, I am with you always, to the end of the age."
> MATTHEW 28:16-20

What are your first reactions to these verses? Why?

In what ways has this commission been carried out in the centuries since Jesus sent His earliest disciples?

In what ways is Jesus' commission still incomplete?

The Great Commission summarized Jesus' mission not only for His earliest disciples, but for all of the disciples who have joined the ranks of His followers throughout history—including you. We'll conclude this study by taking a close look at Jesus' commission and command for those who choose to follow Him.

UNPACK THE STORY

JESUS TELLS US WHERE TO GO

The first thing to highlight about Jesus' statements in these verses is His claim to authority. Why is it important that "all authority has been given to [Jesus] in heaven and on earth"? Because His Great Commission is a series of commands. He is ordering us to obey Him. Therefore, He first wanted to state clearly that He carries the authority to do so.

What does it mean to recognize Jesus' authority in our lives?

Next, the Great Commission has a geographical connection. Jesus commanded us to "Go, therefore, and make disciples of all nations." Notice that Jesus' command is active rather than passive. He didn't command His disciples to think about the world. He didn't ask His followers to say nice things about different people groups. Jesus commanded His disciples to "Go."

> Jesus' command is active rather than passive. He didn't command His disciples to think about the world. He didn't ask His followers to say nice things about different people groups. Jesus commanded His disciples to "Go."

This doesn't mean all Christians should abandon their jobs, leave their families, and serve as international missionaries. However, it does mean all Christians should take an active role in spreading the gospel throughout the world—and it certainly means we should be open to the possibility of physically traveling to other places to spread the gospel.

How would you describe your experiences with missions?

Notice also that Jesus' command involves "all nations." Jesus died for the sins of all people, which means the gospel has power for every tribe and nationality across the world. We cannot forget that Jesus has commanded us, His disciples, to proclaim the gospel message to all who need to hear it.

To ignore the spiritual needs of people outside our own country is to disobey the Great Commission and ignore what Christ has commanded.

What are different ways we can obey Jesus and contribute to spreading the gospel across "all nations"?

JESUS TELLS US WHAT TO DO

Not only did Jesus tell us where to participate in His mission, He also gave us a clear process through which we can carry out that mission:

> [19] "Go, therefore, and make disciples of all nations, baptizing them in the name of the Father and of the Son and of the Holy Spirit, [20] teaching them to observe everything I have commanded you."
> MATTHEW 28:19-20

This process is key to understanding our mission as followers of Jesus. We are called to make disciples, and we start by proclaiming the gospel wherever we can. When our efforts produce fruit—when someone makes a decision to follow Jesus—baptism is the next step. To be baptized is to publicly announce yourself as a follower of Christ.

How would you describe baptism to an unbeliever?

Unfortunately, many Christians believe this to be the end of the process—that once a person "gets saved" and is baptized, there's nothing left to do. Jesus told us differently in His Great Commission. When we proclaim the gospel and engage the process of making disciples, we are responsible for "teaching them to observe everything" He has commanded us.

Certainly this kind of "teaching" involves helping people learn information about God and His Word—but it also goes way beyond information. When we teach people to "observe" what Jesus commanded, we teach them to obey. And the only real way to teach obedience is to model what needs to be obeyed. In other words, one of our main goals in living out the Great Commission is to connect with new disciples in such a way that we provide an example of how to follow Christ.

One of our main goals in living out the Great Commission is to connect with new disciples in such a way that we provide an example of how to follow Christ.

Who has been an example of Christlikeness for you?

How confident do you feel in your ability to make disciples and serve as an example for others to follow?

ENGAGE

When Christians think about Jesus' command to "make disciples of all nations," we often get stuck on the idea of physically traveling to foreign lands. That is certainly part of what Jesus meant, and it is important for us to keep an open mind about full-time and part-time missions work. However, there are many other ways to engage the mission of making disciples throughout the world.

For example, prayer is one of the best tools available for joining Jesus in His mission for the nations. Prayer is both easily accessible and powerfully effective. It can't be stopped by restricted borders or corrupt governments. And prayer works in our lives, as well, to keep us connected with God.

Take a minute to practice praying for the nations as a group. To get started, look on the tag of your shirt—or your shoes, if that's easier—to see in which country it was manufactured. Use the following guidelines to pray for God's kingdom to move forward in that country.

Pray for the churches and Christians currently living in your selected country. Pray for their safety and their ability to share the gospel.

Pray against any corruption or religious persecution that threatens your fellow disciples.

Pray for new opportunities to share the gospel in your country and to meet the needs of those who live there.

PRAYER REQUESTS

....

....

....

....

....

1. Thomas Fields-Meyer, "Organ Transplants: Can a New Heart Change Your Life—and Your Taste in Music?" *People* magazine, vol. 63, no. 13, 04 April 2005. Available from the Internet: *people.com*.

In addition to studying God's Word, work with your group leader to create a plan for personal study, worship, and application between now and the next session. Select from the following optional activities to match your personal preferences and available time.

⬆ Worship

☑ Read your Bible. Complete the reading plan on page 168.

☐ Spend time with God by engaging the devotional experience on page 169.

☐ Connect with God each day through prayer. Ask Him to provide opportunities for you to participate in His mission of making disciples.

➡ ⬅ Personal Study

☐ Read and interact with "Jesus Tells Us Where to Go" on page 170.

☐ Read and interact with "Jesus Tells Us What to Do" on page 172.

⬅ ➡ Application

☐ Make an effort this week to connect with and interact with people who have not experienced salvation through Jesus Christ. Break your normal routines and make a concerted effort to engage in a spiritual conversation.

☐ Make a list of people in your life whom Jesus may be leading you to disciple. Pray through that list each day.

☐ Make a list of people who would be good candidates to disciple you (or to serve as a mentor). Pray through that list each day.

☐ Memorize Acts 1:8: "But you will receive power when the Holy Spirit has come on you, and you will be my witnesses in Jerusalem, in all Judea and Samaria, and to the end of the earth."

☐ Other:

WORSHIP

READING PLAN

Read through the following Scripture passages this week. Use the space provided to record your thoughts and responses.

Day 1
Mark 16:1-20

Day 2
Luke 10:1-16

Day 3
Luke 24:36-53

Day 4
John 20:1-31

Day 5
Romans 10:1-21

Day 6
Romans 16:1-27

Day 7
2 Corinthians 10:1-18

THE FEAR OF FAILING

Our fears often hold us back from obeying Jesus and fulfilling His Great Commission. We can become fearful of many things, such as:

- Looking foolish.
- Not knowing the answers to questions.
- Being rejected.
- Being called out for our own sin, and much more.

Basically, we're afraid of failing. And these fears aren't irrational. In fact, these and other fears will come true time and time again if we commit to making disciples. We will be rejected. We may look foolish even to ourselves. We'll trip and fall over the truth. But remember this truth: We never fail when we choose to obey God. This is true even when we don't have all of the "right" answers—even when we're rejected, scorned, neglected, and despised.

In fact, when we're rejected and despised, we're a lot like Jesus.

On the other hand, never forget that to abandon our commission—to refuse to go, share, give, and speak—is to have already failed. We don't have to be the ones who control the outcome and change people's hearts. All we have to do is obediently go as our Savior sends us out. The choice is ours.

> *What makes you feel afraid at the thought of sharing the gospel with the people in your life?*

> *When has fear prevented you from fulfilling Jesus' commission?*

> *What specific steps will you take to own your fears and overcome them?*

JESUS TELLS US WHERE TO GO

We know that Jesus has called us to join Him in a crucial mission: the redemption of the world. We also know He has the authority to call us into action:

> Jesus came near and said to them, "All authority has been given to me in heaven and on earth."
> MATTHEW 28:18

To have authority means having the power to give orders to others—and having the ability to see those orders carried out to completion. In other words, someone with authority can both enact and enforce a decree. Therefore, Jesus' claim to authority means He can send us out into the world.

But here's the great news: Jesus' authority also means we carry His power and credentials when we go out into the world to do His work. In other words, we aren't proclaiming the gospel and making disciples based on our own names or our own abilities. Instead, we've been sent by the One who holds the keys to both heaven and earth.

This takes the pressure off of us because Jesus is the One who makes things happen. Jesus is the One who changes hearts, minds, and habits. Jesus is the One who convicts people of their sin. Jesus is the One who redeems the world. All we need to do is be faithful to obey His command: "Go."

Have you been relying on Jesus' authority or on your own abilities during your efforts to make disciples?

1	2	3	4	5	6	7	8	9	10

My own abilities   Jesus' authority

What steps can you take to lean more heavily on Jesus' authority?

Now that we understand the basic question of authority behind Jesus' command to "Go," we must still obey Jesus' commission. In Matthew 28, He called the disciples to "make disciples of all nations." Immediately before His ascension, Jesus clarified the different places we should go in our efforts to make disciples.

⁷ He said to them, "It is not for you to know times or periods that the Father has set by his own authority. ⁸ But you will receive power when the Holy Spirit has come on you, and you will be my witnesses in Jerusalem, in all Judea and Samaria, and to the end of the earth."
ACTS 1:7-8

In what ways do you need the Holy Spirit to help you bear witness to your "Jerusalem," "Judea," "Samaria," and "to the end of the earth"?

The places Jesus referenced move outward geographically. They start in close proximity and move further away. Jerusalem was the place closest to where Jesus spoke these words; it was the central city for both the Jews and the earliest Christians. Judea was the name of the region that included cities like Jerusalem, Bethlehem, and Joppa. It was a broader area. Samaria was the region to the north, and it was noteworthy because the Samaritan people and the Jews were enemies—they were different in terms of ethnicity and religion.

You probably don't live in any of those places, but Jesus' call still applies to you. How? Your "Jerusalem" includes the people closest to you; it's your family, friends, neighbors, and coworkers. Your "Judea" is your larger community, including the people in your county, state, and country. Your "Samaria" is the people who are around you but not like you—those who are different from you.

Finally, don't ignore Jesus' command to be witnesses "to the end of the earth." All disciples of Christ have a responsibility to think internationally as we follow Him and make disciples.

Who are some people you can serve from the following groups?

Your "Jerusalem":

Your "Judea":

Your "Samaria":

"The end of the earth":

JESUS TELLS US WHAT TO DO

We've seen that Jesus gave us the process through which we can participate in His mission for the world by making disciples of all nations:

> [19] Go, therefore, and make disciples of all nations, baptizing them in the name of the Father and of the Son and of the Holy Spirit, [20] teaching them to observe everything I have commanded you. And remember, I am with you always, to the end of the age.
> MATTHEW 28:19-20

The process involves four steps:

1. **Go.** We go into the world to sow the seeds of the gospel through our words and deeds.

2. **Make disciples.** When the Holy Spirit causes those seeds to grow in the lives of those we know, we help them respond to God through repentance.

3. **Baptize them.** We help new disciples connect with the body of Christ through the public declaration of their faith.

4. **Teach them to observe Jesus' commands.** We walk in partnership with new disciples to help them learn the truths of God's Word, apply those truths, and begin making disciples themselves.

Which of these steps do you find most difficult or intimidating? Why?

As members of the church, we often feel as if our "job" is done when a person reaches step 3 and makes a public declaration of faith in Jesus. It's not.

To be sure, what we refer to as "salvation" or "justification" is an incredible moment in the life of a disciple—it's the moment during which a person moves from death into life. Likewise, baptism is a wonderful event that should be celebrated by all members of the church.

However, there is much more work to be done. Our commission from Jesus involves continually teaching new and established disciples what it means to follow Him. We are commanded to participate in the sanctification of others even as we experience sanctification ourselves.

Use the questions below to help you think about your own journey through the process of discipleship. Also work to identify the ways you're investing in this process today in the lives of others.

How have you benefited from other followers of Jesus during each of these four steps?

Go:

Make disciples:

Baptize them:

Teach them:

How are you currently helping others follow Jesus through each of these four steps?

Go:

Make disciples:

Baptize them:

Teach them:

REFLECT AND CONNECT

Finish Volume 1 with a time of review
and fellowship as a group.

REFLECT

In the previous session, your group took a deeper look at Jesus' Great Commission for His disciples. You've seen that following Jesus means actively going where He wants us to go and intentionally doing whatever He asks us to do—including sharing the gospel message with those who need to hear it.

Which of the assignments did you explore this week? How did it go?

What did you learn or experience while reading the Bible?

What questions would you like to ask?

As you conclude Volume 1 of *Disciples Path: The Journey,* use this final session as an opportunity to review what you've learned and enjoy spending time together as a community. When helpful, use the following questions to help guide your conversations.

What's something big happening in your life right now?

How has your participation in this group been a positive influence on your spiritual life?

What's a "next step" you are currently pursuing as a disciple of Christ?

PRAY

Conclude this session with an extended time of prayer as a group. Allow each member an opportunity to share both praises and requests for intercession. Conclude by praying together in whatever method is most comfortable for your group.